T0276979

THINKING
IN A
PANDEMIC

a copublication of
BOSTON REVIEW & VERSO BOOKS

made possible by a generous grant from
THE WILLIAM AND FLORA HEWLETT FOUNDATION

CONTENTS

EDITOR'S NOTE
Matt Lord

NOVEMBER 2, 2020

NEARLY A YEAR after the first COVID-19 cases were detected in late 2019, the toll of the coronavirus pandemic is grim. Globally, the disease has directly claimed over a million lives—more than 225,000 in the United States alone. Billions of others have been thrown into deep distress, both by the virus itself and by efforts to contain it.

In many places, the numbers are only getting worse. As I write, the number of new cases has set a daily record in the United States, the daily number of hospitalizations is on its third upswing since April, and several European countries have imposed some form of a second national lockdown. Meanwhile, following successful campaigns at containment—some deeply controversial—life in many Asian countries has more or less returned to normal.

But numbers do not tell the whole story. As months of protests and polarization over pandemic response have made clear, COVID-19 is not just a public health crisis: it is also a crisis of public reason. In a political climate already plagued by misinformation and historically low levels of trust in government, controversy has erupted over every facet of coronavirus research, from masks and mathematical models to data and drugs. The World Health Organization speaks of fighting not just the epidemic but an "infodemic" alongside it.

We should not mistake public controversy for expert disagreement, of course. Epidemiological consensus has converged on the importance of masks, contact tracing, mass testing, and social distancing—all key elements of responses in Asia. But the injunction to "follow the science" misrepresents the full complexity of scientific practice, especially where it intersects with political power and while it is being reshaped by the exigencies of COVID-19.

Science is more than settled theories and static facts: it is a dynamic institution. It is also not singular but plural—more than one field, more than one voice, more than one result—and its claims must be carefully reviewed, balanced, and communicated. Early inconsistencies in messaging about masks on the part of public health authorities—and the change of course prompted by democratic scrutiny of their arguments—reveal just how much public reasoning matters. "In a functioning democracy," Sheila Jasanoff writes in her 2012 book *Science and Public Reason*, "there has to be a correspondence between what officials offer in the way of public justification and what is heard and respected by the citizens."

In short, there is no royal road from expertise to action. What do we know, and how should we act? We cannot answer without public reasoning about which evidence counts, which arguments are valid, and which interventions are justified. Highly sensitive to the actions of powerful experts and ordinary citizens alike, this elaborate exercise in knowledge production, public policy, and democratic deliberation shapes the lives of billions.

The essays in this volume—from epidemiologists and physicians, philosophers and historians, anthropologists and social scientists—were written on the front lines of these debates. Drawn from *Boston Review*'s ongoing series Thinking in a Pandemic, they show the public conversation about science and policy unfolding in real time. The essays are organized in three sections. The first, "Pandemic History," sets the stage for COVID-19 by viewing pandemic science and pandemic politics in historical perspective. The second, "Pandemic Philosophy," features an exchange with two prominent epidemiologists on the nature of evidence and the logic of intervention. And the third, "Pandemic Policy," examines five case studies at the interface of science and society, from the health effects of the economic downturn to the implications of racial discrepancies in the workings of pulse oximeters.

The result is an essential record of public thinking about the pandemic. Together the contributors make clear that the challenge of COVID-19 has always been both scientific and social. Only by reasoning collectively about all its facets will we be able to meet it.

PANDEMIC HISTORY

Science,
Politics,
Society

NEW PATHOGEN, OLD POLITICS
Alex de Waal

APRIL 3, 2020

THERE IS A SAYING among epidemiologists: "If you've seen one pandemic, you've seen one pandemic." Echoing this trade wisdom in an interview two weeks ago, Bruce Aylward, the assistant director of the World Health Organization (WHO), pointed out that each new pandemic follows its own logic, and those who rely on past experiences to draw conclusions for public health will make mistakes. With each new pandemic, it is tempting to scour history books for parallels and lessons learned. But as many have stressed, the wisdom to be gained is often greatly exaggerated.

Still, it is possible to steer a course between the Scylla of historical blindness and the Charybdis of hasty generalization. In her book about the Black Death of 1348, *A Distant Mirror* (1978), historian Barbara Tuchman confines her remarks on the present to a few oblique lines in the preface. "If one insists upon a lesson from history," she writes, it is, as the French medievalist Edouard Perroy contended, that "certain ways of behavior, certain reactions against fate, throw mutual light upon each other." My working premise is that although the pathogen may be new, the logic of social response is not, and it is here that we can see historical continuities. An especially telling case study—still an object of fascination and controversy among historians of health and disease—is the devastating outbreak of cholera in Hamburg at the end of the nineteenth century, the subject of Richard Evans's superbly researched *Death in Hamburg* (1987).

On the morning of August 24, 1892, Robert Koch arrived at Hamburg railway station from his laboratory in Berlin. Germany's most famous medical scientist, he was already credited with discovering the anthrax disease cycle and the bacillus that causes tuberculosis. In the 1880s he had traveled to Egypt and India, where he succeeded in isolating the bacterium responsible for cholera, and on his return to Berlin, he was feted by Kaiser Wilhelm, invested with the Order of the Crown, and put in charge of protecting the empire from epidemics of infectious diseases.

Nine days before Koch's train arrived in Hamburg, a doctor in the neighboring town of Altona had been called to see a stricken construction worker, whose job included inspecting the sewage works. He was suffering from acute vomiting and diarrhea; the diagnosis was cholera. In the first sign of the lethal controversy that was just beginning to erupt, the physician's superior medical officer refused to accept the diagnosis. From August 16 to 23, the daily count of cases grew exponentially to more than 300; over the following 6 weeks, some 10,000 residents of Hamburg perished. Like a forest fire racing through dry tinder, the epidemic burned itself out in October, an ending helped by the efforts of Koch and his team.

As we now know, those deaths were totally preventable. The immediate cause of death was *Vibrio cholerae*, but the city authorities were accomplices to mass mortality, having long resisted spending public money on public health and fearing that a declaration of cholera—with the quarantine and isolation sure to follow—would bring their trading city to a halt. In Altona, just outside Hamburg's jurisdiction, there were few infections; in Hamburg's sister port of Bremen, a self-administering former Hanseatic League city-state, there were just six cases, half of them recent arrivals from Hamburg. Hamburg suffered alone that year.

In their pitch and consequence, these events have the narrative structure and moral tensions of a theatrical tragedy. Besides the cholera vibrio itself, which takes the shape of a comma (like its typographical counterpart, potentially catastrophic if inserted at a crucial juncture), the dramatis personae are Koch, chemist and hygienist Max von Pettenkofer, physician-anthropologist Rudolf Virchow, and a chorus of the afflicted themselves and some of their revolutionary spokesmen. There are five subplots. Science contends with superstition and fatalism; the new germ theory of disease disputes with so-called ecological or local conjunctural theories; militarized centralizing bureaucracy spars with liberal capitalism; the anthropocentric "epidemic narrative" that promises a return to the safety of life-as-normal wrestles with the logic of evolution operating on different timescales from the microscopic to the macro-ecological; and last, an open, democratic society questions its limits.

As we will see, some that is old is new again.

Cholera: The Nineteenth Century's Most Fearsome Pandemic

UNTIL THE EARLY NINETEENTH CENTURY, cholera was endemic to the Ganges Delta in Bengal, but it appears not to have been found elsewhere. The causative bacillus lives in warm water and multiplies in the human intestine, transmitted by fecal contamination. That was cholera's macro-ecology: all it needed was to survive in just a few shallow wells during each dry season, with every annual flood spreading the germ far and wide.

Along with the great famine of the 1770s, one of the lethal gifts of the English East India Company was opening up routes whereby cholera could spread far more widely, colonizing new places as a kind of biological blowback. British investment in widespread irrigation to grow cotton created the perfect ecology in which the vibrio could find multiple local reserves—irrigation ditches and canals, reservoirs, wells, water tanks—and become endemic. In 1854 English physician John Snow elegantly demonstrated that the infection was waterborne. He showed this through an epidemiological study still heralded in textbooks today: after painstakingly plotting cases on a London street map, he asked each affected household where it obtained its drinking water, tracing the source to a single contaminated pump on Bow Street.

According to legend, Snow asked the local alderman to remove the handle on the pump, and new cases promptly ceased. In fact, as Snow himself admitted, the epidemic was already subsiding by that time, but he had made his point: the dominant "miasma" explanation—that the disease was caused by locally generated impure air—had a competitor theory that had the virtues of being simple and provable. In the same year that Snow was mapping the outbreak, Florentine microbiologist Filippo Pacini described the bacillus, which he had extracted from the autopsies of victims. But Pacini had no powerful political apparatus behind him to endorse and broadcast his breakthrough, and medical studies were not sufficiently systematic for the correct conclusion to be drawn. Thus the paradigm shift was not automatic. Rather, advocates of the miasma theory refined their arguments, contending that complicated local interactions of soil, air, and personal characteristics accounted for the vagaries of the disease. Prominent among the exponents of these views was indefatigable chemist, hygienist, and health reformer Max von Pettenhofer, whom we shall encounter in Hamburg shortly.

Cholera first reached Europe in 1830, causing mass mortality, panic, and unrest. The vibrio produces particularly nasty symptoms in its human host: once it enters the intestine, its ideal microecology, it multiplies exponentially and drives out the resident microbiota within just a few hours. The stricken body loses control of its functions, lapses into fits of uncontrollable vomiting, diarrhea, and muscle spasms, and turns blue and bloated. Catastrophic dehydration then causes death in about half of those infected.

For the emergent bourgeoisie in Europe, the manner of cholera's attack was no less terrifying than the prospect of mortality: an individual could be stricken at dinner, or in a tramcar, causing revulsion and terror among his or her companions. Just as disturbing to the authorities were "cholera riots" in which peasants and the inhabitants of the newly expanding, grossly unsanitary industrial cities attacked

de Waal

landlords, city authorities, and in some cases physicians, accusing them of using the disease as a pretext for driving them out of their homes and seizing their property. Sometimes the poor even blamed the rich for having introduced the disease for that very purpose.

Subsequent cholera pandemics coincided with the 1848 uprisings throughout Europe—with localized outbreaks for a decade, including the one that prompted Snow's investigation—and the wars of the 1860s. In 1891 famine struck Russia, prompting a wave of migration by hundreds of thousands of people one or two economic steps up from the starving peasantry. The following year, the tsar expelled the Jews from Moscow and the vibrio traveled westward with both groups. Those tired, poor, huddled masses dreamed of the United States, and the Hamburg–America shipping company was the most traveled route to the New World. German health authorities registered the cases as the migrants moved; many were stopped at the border, but some passed through undetected. The epidemic warning lights were blinking red.

Medical and Ecological Controversies, Then and Now

CHOLERA IS A PANTOMIME VILLAIN in this drama: stealthy, sudden, and lethal. At the time of the Hamburg epidemic, there was still much controversy about its etiology. Was it a contaminant invader? Did it emerge when there was a special configuration of local conditions? Thirty years after Snow and Pacini, and eight years after Koch isolated the vibrio, there still wasn't medical unanimity. Hamburg was to change that.

Scientific method was itself developing alongside medical discoveries, and Koch was in the vanguard of both. "Koch's postulates," as we now call them, were criteria for determining whether the agent of a disease had indeed been correctly identified. According to the postulates, the microbiologist had first to identify the suspected microbe in all infected individuals; then it should be grown in culture; third he had to use the microbe to infect an experimental host and observe it sicken with similar symptoms; and finally isolate the same microbe in the sick or deceased animal. The experiment had to be repeatable. Ironically, Koch's identification of the cholera vibrio did not fulfill his own criteria; despite his best efforts, he could not induce cholera in an animal host. It only affects humans. There were also plenty of who, why, and where questions left unanswered about outbreaks—enough material for skeptics to make the case that the germ theory was, at minimum, incomplete.

The cholera controversies of the 1880s and 1890s were, nonetheless, the first conducted under the dawning light of the new microbiology. So-called "anti-contagionists" and "localists" argued that there surely had to be other conducive factors such as the weather, the soil, or the temperament of the individual patient. Radicals asked, why was it that the proletariat were always hardest hit? (Studies of disease patterns show that this wasn't always the case, but it was true often enough to serve as grist for social reform agendas.)

In the case of COVID-19 today, the mysteries are fewer, the scientific method is more robust, and the speed with which controversies are resolved is many times faster. The lapse between identifying a new disease and knowing its pathogen is closer to five days than five decades. The virus was isolated within a few days of the first cases and its entire genome was sequenced and available online two weeks later. We have the benefits of testing and tracing and massive computational power in charting epidemiological scenarios. Still, much remains uncertain, and epidemiologists continue to revise their understanding of the case fatality rate and vulnerability factors. We do not know whether COVID-19 will infect 20 percent, 40 percent, or 70 percent of the population. It is important to parse our ignorance, separating out what risk is calculable now, what risk will be calculated when we have better data, and what is profoundly uncertain because it cannot be captured by data gathering.

Consider an example. In their influential modeling of possible trajectories and the impact of "non-pharmacological interventions" (NPIs, by which they mean policies such as quarantine or social distancing), Neil Fergusson and colleagues at Imperial College London include the following caveats:

> It is important to note at the outset that given SARS-CoV-2 is a newly emergent virus, much remains to be understood about its transmission. In addition, the impact of many of the NPIs detailed here depends critically on how people respond to their introduction, which is highly likely to vary between countries and even communities. Last, it is highly likely that there would be significant spontaneous changes in population behaviour even in the absence of government-mandated interventions.

There are two caveats here, and they should be treated differently. The first is that the basic data for sound epidemiology are not yet known, but better approximations are constantly becoming available. This is an exercise in better calculation of risk. The second caveat, which Fergusson divides into two, is that outcomes will depend upon how people respond, both to official policies and because of other changing beliefs. Health behavior is harder to measure than epidemiological constants. The point is that the *social* component of the trajectory of the epidemic is uncertain in a way the *medical* component is not: although the margins can be narrowed, the risk really cannot be quantified. In a series of blog posts examining the intersection of health, environment, and politics, scholar of science and technology policy Andy Stirling explains "the crucial distinction between 'uncertainty' and 'risk.' A risk is what results from a structured calculation that must necessarily reflect a particular view. An 'uncertainty' is what these risk calculations might leave out." Health behavior is just one part of this.

Another element of uncertainty is that epidemics are inflection points in evolution across different scales from the microbial to the planetary. Pathogens evolve; microbes populate the microbiomes of animals and plants, the soil and the water; remnants of viruses are found in our DNA. For bacteria and viruses, the boundaries of the human self hold no meaning, and the more that we discover about the viral remnants in our DNA and the richness of our microbiomes, the more we are compelled to acknowledge that point of view. The vicious nineteenth-century strains of cholera retained their prior strategy of rapidity and lethality, killing about half of the humans they colonized. In the mid-twentieth century, the "El Tor" strain evolved a new strategy of lower virulence. This is a common adaptive trajectory for pathogens, which prosper by treating their hosts as symbiotes instead of wantonly destroying them. The first pandemic of any new pathogen is, for the human population, usually the worst—so it was for bubonic plague in Asia and Europe, smallpox and measles in the Americas, and cholera. It is no solace to *Homo sapiens* facing COVID-19 today.

Ecosystems change too. Most of the new pathogens that infect humans are zoonotic: they jump the species barrier, from wild monkeys or bats, or from domesticated chickens or pigs. This has always been the case. But in the past, a zoonotic pathogen might infect a band of hunter-gatherers; today, thanks to a globalized, deeply interconnected world, a single local outbreak can become a pandemic in a few weeks. Another new factor is the proximity of humans to domestic animals and factory farms. The 90 percent of nonhuman terrestrial vertebrate biomass on the planet husbanded for our consumption lives—if we can call it living—in ecosystems such as feedlots that have no precedent. These are perfect incubators for new zoonoses, especially for avian influenza, which can evolve first in chickens, then jump to pig populations that act as a kind of pathogenic evolutionary accelerator, and finally make the leap to humans. In turn, each new human–pathogen dyad alters the ecology of global public health and disease: our built environment changes (in the nineteenth century with the introduction of municipal water supplies, for example); our biochemical environment changes (supplementing animal feed with antibiotics, for example); and our health behaviors change. Meanwhile, climate change is altering the ecologies of infectious diseases in ways that we cannot predict. The post-pandemic world is a changed ecosystem.

Though a great deal of headway has been made into the study of these complex environmental factors, the uncertainties they introduce are left out of epidemiological models narrowly focused on predicting numbers of cases and deaths. The standard "epidemic narrative" consists of a stable "normality" threatened by the intrusion of a novel, alien pathogenic threat, followed by an epidemic and an epidemic response (of variable proficiency) and ends with a return to the status quo ante. That neat storyline simply isn't going to happen. In turn, in Hamburg 140 years ago and across the world today, what is "left out" depends on where you stand.

How Liberals Failed to Prevent Epidemics

SO MUCH FOR the microbial protagonist. Let's turn now to the three human characters in our retelling of the Hamburg tragedy.

First on stage is the dominating and ultimately tragic figure of Max von Pettenkofer (1818–1901)—almost unknown today, but 130 years ago at the height of his professional fame as Germany's preeminent chemist. He championed medical research, advocated clean air and urban sanitation, and mentored dozens of students. In the comic book version of our Hamburg story, though, all these achievements count for naught: he is instead the villain whose obstinate pride, reprised by his acolytes who dominated Hamburg's medical policies, failed the people of that city twice over. Their biggest shortcoming was failing to prepare for waterborne diseases and refusing to order the construction of filtration plants to treat the city's drinking water so that people were drinking water piped straight from the river Elbe to storage tanks, and from there to their homes. As water levels dropped in the dry, hot summer of 1892, contaminants were washed by the tides and currents from riverside towns and from the barges that plied the waterway. Filtering through sand efficiently removes *Vibrio cholerae*. Other cities did it; Hamburg did not.

Why did Hamburg authorities take this stance? Despite the centralizing ambitions of the Prussian state, and the uniform color of its territories on the political map of Europe, the administration of Germany was not yet unified. Hamburg, the second-largest city and its richest port, still retained the legacy of self-government from its membership in the Hanseatic League. The city was run by its own senate and zealously guarded its powers to make independent policy decisions, especially in matters of trade. Indeed, Hamburg was the most "English" city in Germany, governed by an assembly of its citizens—by its constitution, a small and privileged group of property owners; by its social history, an oligarchy of traders and lawyers. They disliked and distrusted the military–bureaucratic Prussian ways of state.

Those citizens believed in small government, balancing the books, and individual responsibility for health and well-being. Spending their tax money on a filtration plant looked to be an extravagance that threatened both the fiscal health of the city-state and the ethic by which it had prospered. These laissez-faire doctrines resembled those that had led Britain to the utmost parsimony in famine relief in Ireland and India—its colonial administrators holding fast to the belief that public debt was a more egregious sin than mass starvation, and that the hungry could only remedy their plight through learning the self-discipline of hard work and husbanding scarce resources.

The next-biggest failing of von Pettenkofer's loyal disciples in Hamburg—especially chief medical officer Dr. Johann Kraus—was their refusal to accept the cholera diagnoses and issue a cholera declaration during those crucial days in August when the rate of infection was doubling each day. As we have now learned once again, to our collective cost, bacilli and viruses can multiply exponentially. The delay of a day can make the difference between containing an outbreak and facing an epidemic.

Why did they not do this? Part of the explanation is the intellectual inflexibility of men of high standing. The other part is material interest. Port that it is, in the 1890s Hamburg's economy, and the prosperity of its plutocrats, depended on keeping the harbor open and the ships moving. Goods were coming in from England and the United States. The larger part of Germany's exports was arriving by barge and train to be loaded onto ships destined for every continent, and the Hamburg–America line had regular sailings for New York, the decks packed with migrants seeking a better life on the far shore of the Atlantic.

If we read von Pettenkofer's calculation as a straightforward tradeoff between profit and human life, we do him an injustice. Most of the public health measures to deal with cholera began as hand-me-downs from the medieval plagues, revised during the previous sixty years during the visitations of cholera, adapted each time based on a rule-of-thumb empirical assessment of what had worked and what hadn't. New viruses and bacilli had emerged; society's responses stayed much the same.

The first draft of the plague control playbook was drawn up in Italian city-states in the years after the apocalyptic shock of the 1348 Black Death. Much like cholera half a millennium later, the plague arrived explosively and killed in a gruesome and rapid way. Its mortality was extraordinarily high: overall, perhaps a third of the population of Asia and Europe succumbed, and in most European cities, half of residents perished, sometimes in just a few weeks.

The calamity was widely attributed to divine wrath, astronomical alignments, witchcraft, and sorcery. Italian princes, city elders, and merchants were more empirical. The first boards of health were set up in Venice and Florence in the same year that the plague appeared; these evolved into permanent magistracies over the next century, with authority to restrict travel and trade, and isolate infected individuals. Isolation hospitals, called *lazzaretti*, were set up to prevent contagion. Italian cities also issued certificates of health to important traders and diplomats, so that they could pass freely through checkpoints. The first passports were health cards.

Observing that the plague tended to appear first on ships from the East and then spread when those ships arrived in port, they began comparing notes and drawing up advice. Quarantine was first trialed in the Venetian port of Ragusa (now Dubrovnik) in 1377—its name refers to the forty days that suspected vessels were kept offshore to see if sailors and passengers fell sick. Within a few decades, the fundamentals of plague control had been worked out by trial and error: alongside quarantine, what we would now call notification of cases of infection, isolation of the sick, imposition of *cordons sanitaires* and travel restrictions, and disinfection (usually through burning the property of those infected). The main item missing from the list was carrier control: the role of rats—to be precise, rat fleas—as the reservoir of infection was not known, and systematic suppression of rat infestations was never contemplated, and presumably would have been considered impractical if it had been. Instead, people assumed that plague spread by human-to-human contagion.

The tools of plague containment were part of the scaffolding of the earliest administrative apparatus of the modern European state, and notably so in northern Italy. The science was somewhere between wrong and inexact, the motives mixed, the implementation quite often haphazard. Little wonder that critics condemned these measures as expensive, ineffective, and dangerous. The financial costs hardly need to be restated: the bureaucrats had to be paid, and interruptions to trade caused mercantile bankruptcies. Effectiveness could be questioned: the plague often managed to get through the defenses, and people would find ways of evading the restrictions or overwhelming the policemen dispatched to enforce them. The danger lay in the social unrest that followed unemployment, high food prices, and the intrusions of the police.

It wasn't until 1894 that the pathogen was identified, simultaneously by Alexandre Yersin (a former laboratory assistant at the Pasteur Institute in Paris) and Japanese biochemist Shabasaburo Kitasato (who had trained under Koch in Berlin). They both isolated the microbial cause, a pathogen carried by rat fleas called *Pasteurella pestis* or *Yersinia pestis*—a victory for European science over Asian, and for France over Germany. Plague remained endemic in India and China at that time with sporadic outbreaks, but had vanished from Europe (the last epidemic occurred in Marseille in 1720). Exactly why plague disappeared from Europe remains one of the enduring mysteries of microbial history: was it changes in the rat population, in the ecology of the transmission zones on the eastern borderlands of the continent, or the effectiveness of Europe's quarantines and *lazzaretti*?

The best-documented cases of the plague response toolkit are naturally the most recent, and a good (or bad) example was Bombay in 1896, which is germane to the Hamburg drama for two reasons. First, it illustrates the standard epidemic containment policies as deployed in the same decade. Second, it occurred two years *after* the Yersin/Kitasato breakthrough had revealed that the main mode of transmission was fleas-to-human rather than human-to-human.

Despite the scientific discovery, British officers of the Indian Civil Service remained convinced that the plague endured chiefly due to Indian backwardness. Historian Rajnarayan Chandavarkar observes that even though the medical and scientific experts were up to date on the most recent discoveries, their "policies, formulated on the assumption that the plague was a virulently infectious disease, proved at best oppressive and at worst fatal." Among these, "stringent inspections" on the railroads turned up few cases, while "pumping the sewers with disinfectants" simply drove rats and the fleas they carried into houses, where they promptly spread the infection. The disorderly, distrustful, and sometimes violent response of Bombay residents, dismissed as superstition by colonial officers, is perfectly understandable. The official cure—if indeed it can be counted as such—was arguably as bad as the disease.

Bombay also shows that von Pettenkofer was not alone in disputing the latest medical claims. Indeed, Hamburg was following well-established British precedent in downplaying the modes of transmission of pathogens when commerce was at stake. After the opening of the Suez Canal in 1869, the International Cholera Control Commission in Istanbul insisted that British ships with infected sailors or passengers be kept at sea for the requisite forty days, bringing the (French-led) commission into conflict with ministers in London, who insisted that quarantine regulations were a gross violation of the 1846 Free Trade Act. Influential English doctors insisted that the germ theory of cholera was "a humbug got up for the restriction of our commerce." Until March 2020 at least, British public health policy retained a laissez-faire strand quite distinct from continental Europe.

Von Pettenkofer's doctrines are thus much more comprehensible in the context of these centuries of practice in epidemic control with limited outcomes, the oppressive aspects of quarantine and isolation, and the uncertainties of the medical science and epidemiology of the time. His medical and social beliefs were an odd mélange; he is hard to place in today's political spectrum. He advocated "localism," believing in particular that cholera became virulent only in particular kinds of soil, and that it needed a human body with the requisite moral and psychological preconditions to develop into the full-blown disease. He held that health was a matter for individual family responsibility, not state diktat.

In our drama, the first fatal error of von Pettenkofer's followers began as a relatively minor fault, amplified by their inflexibility. They steadfastly refused to purify Hamburg's drinking water by the relatively straightforward method of filtering it through sand, which efficiently removes the cholera vibrio. Von Pettenkofer could readily have accommodated the cleansing powers of sand into his general promotion of cleanliness and his view that the bacillus also needed a receptive soil to become potentially lethal. But almost as if gripped by a death wish, he took a stand that water filtration was a needless expense without benefit. In our drama, we can imagine the audience silently urging him: "Just filter the water supply! *Just do it!*"

The second disastrous error, directly attributable to his student Kraus, was the refusal to declare a cholera epidemic on August 18, 1892, or over the following few days. Only on August 23, the day before Koch arrived, did Hamburg medical authorities admit that the disease was present in their city. By that time, every part of the city was affected.

The denouement of von Pettenkofer's role occurs when his students have been driven out of their posts, but he still rancorously defends his "local configuration" theory. He lays down the ultimate challenge to Koch: he will drink a solution containing the cholera vibrio and see what happens. The old man did this on October 7, 1892, recording the grotesque symptoms in his diary. He recovered, concluding that his view was vindicated: cholera needed both an infectious agent and also a conducive host. An identical experiment was undertaken by his disciple Rudolf Emmerich ten days later, which he performed on a stage in front of an audience of over a hundred people. Emmerich also survived. (Evans, in *Death in Hamburg*, suggests that Koch's laboratory assistants, who provided the samples, suspected the purpose of the request and mercifully diluted the solutions.) Von Pettenkofer finally fulfilled his death wish with a pistol to his temple in 1901.

How the Centralizers—and Their Science—Prevailed

THE HAMBURG EPIDEMIC occurred at the inflection point in the rise of scientific medicine. The protagonist of this paradigm shift, the hero of the tale, is Koch (1843–1910): he is the one remembered for having taken charge of Hamburg's failing public health system and clearing out the charlatans. When Koch arrived on the train from Berlin on the morning of August 24, carrying the Kaiser's writ, he already knew the diagnosis was cholera; a doctor from Altona had arrived at his laboratory a few days earlier with a sealed jar containing samples from patients. But he apparently had no idea of how rapidly the disease had taken hold nor how negligent was the municipal response.

There was no official delegation at the railway station to meet the empire's highest-ranking scientist. Koch had to make his own plans: his first stop was the city medical office, where he arrived at nine in the morning. Kraus turned up only thirty minutes later, and had little information to impart, for he had done nothing other than sneer at the "hyperactive behavior" of his counterparts in other towns (such as Altona). Koch's next stop was the New General Hospital in Eppendorf, where the director, Dr. Theodor Rumpf, was ready to greet him at the door. Koch asked straightaway if there were cholera cases to report, and Rumpf promptly gave him the figures, whereupon Koch remarked to his companion, "The first man in Hamburg who's telling us the truth!"

After visiting the hospitals, disinfection centers, and barracks where the migrants from Russia were housed awaiting their ships,

Koch toured the old, overcrowded, ramshackle "Alley Quarters" in the city center. By this time he was becoming aware that hundreds were already dead. "I felt as if I was walking across a battlefield," he said. And amid these unsanitary streets, courtyards, and canals, he was shocked: "In no other city have I come across such unhealthy dwellings, such plague spots, such breeding places of infection." This was a man who had scoured Alexandria and Calcutta hospitals in his search for the bacterial culprit. In the alleys he made a remark that became an infamous condemnation of Germany's most cosmopolitan city: "Gentlemen," he said, "I forget that I am in Europe."

If any moment in our drama were to mark the shift in the paradigm for understanding epidemic disease, this would be it. This is the point at which the naysayers' defenses became hollow, that the unresolved medical and epidemiological controversies became only minor way stations on the iron railroad of progress, through which the express train of medical science could rush with only a blast of a whistle to warn the loiterers to get out of its way. In more than a metaphorical way, the emperor had arrived on that train.

Recall that when Koch returned from Egypt and India proclaiming that he had discovered the cholera bacillus, there was indeed room for doubt. Koch had not satisfied his own postulates—no animal could be induced to fall sick with cholera—and epidemiological mysteries remained. (When Koch won the Nobel Prize in 1905, the citation was for his discovery of the tuberculosis bacillus, the more complete demonstration of his method.) Kaiser Wilhelm's proclamation of Koch's success was a gamble on science, in the service of imperial politics—he was strenuously seeking to catch up with the other European colonial powers. Seeking what he later called Germany's "place in the sun," he had convened the Berlin Conference that divided Africa among them; his rush to industrialization was gathering pace; his unification of the disparate administrations across the patchwork quilt that had been the principalities, city-states, feudal, and episcopal estates of the former Holy Roman Empire was still incomplete.

At this time and in this context, tropical disease was a huge impediment to colonization, while medicine, especially in France, was justification for empire. The canonization of Koch was a triumph for German medical science, instantly making his laboratory a peer of France's Pasteur Institute. Then as now, scientific competition was interwoven with geostrategic rivalry; it was a matter of both prestige and imperial capability. Health administration, with its requirements of a unified census, border controls, and the machinery of case notification—issuing certificates of good health—required and justified a centralized bureaucracy. Infectious disease reporting and control was not a matter that could be left to the discretion of cities or baronies; unless all parts of the body politic conformed to the same central protocol, the health of the whole would be vulnerable to the deficiencies of its weakest part.

We can see now that Koch's achievement was both scientific and rhetorical. His first scientific achievement was identifying the lifecycle of anthrax, but unable to specify the causal mechanism, he resorted to the persuasive metaphor of "host" and "parasite." He went on to characterize the cholera vibrio as an "invader." And— especially salient with respect to the rivalry between Berlin and

Hamburg—the germ theory of infection was the charter for military centralism over laissez-faire minimal government. On the train from Berlin arrived not just Koch but a freight of martial metaphor, mindset, and mobilizing capacity.

Medicine and the military are indeed deeply entangled throughout recorded history. Armies were epidemics on the march; regiments were depleted more by infection than battle; sailors fell victim to nutritional deficiencies such as scurvy. The scandalous hospital conditions for soldiers during the Crimea War of the 1850s were the occasion for Florence Nightingale to establish British nursing. Biological warfare has long been attempted, though historic successes were due more to chance than design. One account of the plague's entry into Europe was that the Mongol army besieging the Crimean town of Kaffa used catapults to fling infected corpses into the city. The story of the gruesome projectiles may be true, but that is not how plague is transmitted. The Spanish conquest of Mexico was incalculably aided by smallpox, which stowed away on the conquistadors' ships and killed as many as half of the immunologically naïve Native Americans in its first and deadliest epidemic, while leaving the invaders—their faces pockmarked from earlier, immunity-inducing infections—untouched.

None of the above, however, imposed a military model on medicine itself. This changed with the application of modern industrial modes of organization to the organization of war, with the U.S. Civil War and the Franco-Prussian War. These were also the occasions on which modern medicine and the arsenal of epidemic control measures were applied to the same end. Tools of surveillance, standardization, and regimentation were applied equally to state-making, imperial expansion, industrial warfare, and population health. Just as war became about more than conquest, public health was never just about public health.

So too with Koch's visit to Hamburg. The elders of the city had reason to fear that cholera control would jeopardize not just their commerce but also their prized constitutional autonomy. Over the previous decades, while the British Empire had tried to balance health-based controls with free trade, the French had been much more assertive in using the anti-infection arsenal in the service of expanding the writ of the colonial state. Historian Patrick Zylberman recounts how the French government portrayed the disease as an "invasion" from the Levant and India, which justified martial medical measures and the establishment of the outer ramparts of Europe's sanitary frontier in the Middle East.

The authorities in France's Mediterranean ports did not want to require health inspections on arrival, so Paris assembled a coalition of European governments that imposed a regime of health inspection and oversight on the Ottoman Empire. So, even while the Ottomans were nominally independent, western European health officers were stationed in Cairo and Constantinople with the authority to control the westward departure of ships. Zylberman makes the point that the threat of cholera was sufficient justification for "pre-emptive intervention" in the eastern Mediterranean and even beyond: the Ottoman state was the "sick man of Europe" in two senses of the phrase, and the imperialists were already sinking their teeth into its weakening body. Whatever their geostrategic rivalries, Paris and Berlin saw the microbial threat from the East in a similar way: Germany imposed comparable measures along its long land frontiers.

In Hamburg in August 1892, worries about Berlin's militaristic rule and the loss of long-cherished liberties were, of course, less pressing than the terrifying scourge in the water supply. Koch did not declare "war" on the vibrio, and his comparison of the overwhelmed Hamburg hospitals to a "battlefield" was as far as his military metaphors went. Nowhere in the debates of the day do we read political rhetoric of bodily integrity and decay, infection and purification, that was adopted by the Nazis a generation later. But as the militarized Prussian state took over the administration of Hamburg, starting with its hospitals and water supply, the corner was turned.

In the end Koch triumphed over von Pettenkofer; the biomedical paradigm shifted. Centralizing, authoritarian Prussia imposed its ways on liberal Hamburg; Germany's governance system consolidated. Less noticed, the military model of public health became hegemonic. The United States, which watched Hamburg closely—it was, after all, the port where the largest number of immigrants embarked—somehow managed this paradox. The U.S. Army Corps of Engineers became the principal weapon fighting Yellow Fever in Cuba, Louisiana, and Panama alike, while generations of voters have rejected social medicine as either a luxury the country cannot afford or as one step short of totalitarianism.

The metaphor of "fighting" a disease, apt for the body's immune response to a pathogen, is incongruous for the social response to an epidemic. Nonetheless, the language has become so familiar today that it is adopted unreflectingly—a mark of true hegemony. The traffic in metaphors runs both ways. When mobilizing for war or authoritarian measures, political leaders inveigh against "infestation" by invaders or infiltrators that are akin to pathogens. In times of health crisis, they like to "declare war" on a microbial "invisible enemy."

The U.S. Army's medical and engineering corps earned their place in the annals of public health with meticulous research into Yellow Fever transmission, followed by rigorous enforcement of programs of draining, capping, and oiling standing water in wells, cisterns, tanks, and pools; and the use of insecticides to eradicate mosquito-breeding sites. In modern times, and especially since the post-9/11 anthrax scare raised the specter of bioterrorism, so deeply has the U.S. Department of Defense bored into all aspects of U.S. foreign policy that the instrument of choice in responding to diverse crises around the world, including epidemic disease, is the military. The army was the first international provider of relief to Indonesia after the tsunami of 2004 and to Haiti after the earthquake of 2010. President Barack Obama dispatched the 101st Airborne to "fight" Ebola in West Africa in 2014. Today the National Guard and the U.S. Navy have been ordered to the forefront of the COVID-19 emergency response. Military logistics appear to be indispensable in filling the gap of an under-provisioned emergency public health service—though the sight of a nearly empty military hospital ship in New York shows how ill-prepared they are for a civilian epidemic.

However, recognizing the operational role of the military in epidemic response shouldn't seduce us into thinking that security officers and generals should be running the show. The American Civil Liberties Union was alive to this danger, warning in a 2008 report that coercive, law-enforcement approaches would be counterproductive as well as dangerous to rights. Unsurprisingly, the potential for assuming war-time emergency powers and deploying security technologies is attractive to many political leaders precisely because of their dual usage. President Donald Trump has decided to describe himself as a "wartime president." He is following French president Emmanuel Macron who declared "war" on the virus. In Italy it is more of a police operation. Hungary's Viktor Orbán has passed a law allowing him to rule by decree indefinitely and is blaming the pandemic on immigrants and refugees. In China the lockdown is enforced by a combination of high-tech surveillance and old-fashioned Communist Party neighborhood mobilization—a "grid reaction." In Israel the government is proposing to deploy tracking technologies designed to follow terrorists against people believed to be infected with coronavirus. The *Economist* has coined the word "coronopticon" for such all-pervasive surveillance.

Activist Reformers and Silent Revolutionaries

THE WAVE OF REPRESSIVE MEASURES enacted in response to COVID-19 would come as no surprise to the cast of our Hamburg drama. Europe's nineteenth-century cholera epidemics marched in synchrony with its revolutions, notably in 1830–32 and 1848. "Cholera riots" were widespread. In 1892 mobs rampaged through the Russian cities of Astrakhan, Tashkent, Saratov, and Donetsk. The cries of the afflicted provide the chorus to the protagonists, with a handful of spokesmen's voices audible above the shouts and cries. But we would listen in vain for socialist revolutionaries.

Karl Marx was lodging at 28 Dean Street in Soho in 1854, five minutes' walk from the famed Broad Street pump (according to Google Maps) and a minute from the nearest black (infected) dot on John Snow's map in Meard Street. But he made only passing reference to the outbreak in his correspondence with Friedrich Engels, blaming it on poor housing. Engels had done the same in his 1845 book *The Conditions of the Working Class in England*, and in his preface to the 1892 edition added the line:

> Again, the repeated visitations of cholera, typhus, small-pox, and other epidemics have shown the British bourgeois the urgent necessity of sanitation in his towns and cities, if he wishes to save himself and family from falling victims to such diseases. Accordingly, the most crying abuses described in this book have either disappeared or have been made less conspicuous.

Engels, it seems, quietly concedes that public health is a bourgeois science, and an effective one. For the communists, war and class war were the locomotives of history, and microbes had merely hitched a ride. As historian Samuel Cohn observes, this is a baffling surrender of a political battlefield where they could have outflanked their class enemies. "An analysis of cholera and its social consequences did not enter any of Marx's works published in his lifetime," he notes, "and he appears to have been oblivious to any manifestations of its social protest and class struggle." He continues:

Still more surprising is an absence of attention to cholera's social violence by more recent historians of the New Left who have studied nineteenth- and twentieth-century class struggle meticulously—E.P. Thompson, Eric Hobsbawm, John Foster, John Calhoun, and others—despite these events sparking crowds estimated as high as 30,000, taking control of cities (even if only briefly), murdering governors, mayors, judges, physicians, pharmacists, and nurses, destroying factories and towns.

The oversight has begun to be remedied. Postcolonial historians and medical anthropologists have explored local resistance to colonial health policies and the suspicions that surround, among other things, polio vaccination programs. But still there is relatively little research on resistance to public health measures during epidemic emergencies. This is a gap, because each historical visitation of epidemic disease and its corresponding government measures was met with innumerable acts of everyday evasion and noncompliance.

In Italy in the sixteenth and seventeenth centuries, and most memorably in London in 1665, chroniclers of the plague have written about the reckless indifference of poor people to the dangers of contagion, and their subversion of whatever sanitary measures were imposed upon them. Daniel Defoe, like others who wrote on this subject, attributed this behavior to illiteracy, obstinacy, and fatalism. It may also have been a preference for accepting uncertainty (the lottery of the microbe) over the predictable hardship (destitution by unemployment). There are also intriguing echoes with colonized people's resistance to imperial health and environmental diktat, which was usually arbitrary, unscientific, and often achieved nothing beyond a display of state power.

Nineteenth-century socialists' silence on public health is doubly puzzling because their rivals on the left, the radical democrats, were vocal. In the 1848 "springtime of the peoples," while Marx and Engels were writing the Communist Manifesto, a young physician named Rudolf Virchow (1821–1902) was compiling a report on an outbreak of typhus in Silesia. Virchow came to be known both as the father of pathology and the founder of social medicine, but he was also a pioneering physical anthropologist; his studies of the size and shapes of the crania of different people made him conclude that there was no scientific basis for claims of racial superiority or inferiority. His medical practice radicalized his politics; his report on Silesia argued that medical interventions alone had little value, but rather social advancement through education, democracy, and prosperity. Virchow joined the 1848 uprisings as a democrat, with the slogan, "Medicine is a social science, and politics is nothing but medicine at scale."

Like many erudite men of science of the era, Virchow's medical views are hard to classify today. He was generally sympathetic to von Pettenkofer, though disagreed with him on cholera, which he considered a contagion; he admired Koch, though, oddly enough, disputed the role of the tuberculosis bacillus. Fundamentally, Virchow was a libertarian who believed that democracy, education, and progress would eliminate disease. Evans credits him with the crucial insight: "What Virchow's theories made explicit was the indissoluble connection between medical science, economic interest, and political ideology."

Virchow's voice in the Hamburg chorus poses questions that resonate today. Contemporary liberals (in the U.S. usage of the word) are discomfited by the politics of pandemic. They lean toward social health on the grounds of equity but shudder when epidemiological risk management through quarantine and travel restrictions aligns with racist exclusionary policies. U.S. liberals are reassured by the civil servants dedicated to science—Anthony Fauci, director of the National Institute of Allergy and Infectious Diseases, is today's paragon of the virtuous deep state—but disturbed by the totalitarian implications of disease surveillance and control. The infection-control state is Max Weber's military–bureaucratic state on steroids, requiring uniform sanitary habits throughout the population.

In *Disease and Democracy* (2005), Peter Baldwin describes how, in the later twentieth century, as chronic, noninfectious, and "lifestyle" diseases took over from infectious diseases as the main threats to health in industrialized countries, responsibility for health was shifted from states to citizens: "every man his own quarantine officer." Baldwin poses the key question: "Can there be a democratic public health?" He does not think so: "In the era of governmentality, public health remains one clear area of statutory control where the average law-abiding citizen might expect to feel the iron first through the velvet glove."

Baldwin's skepticism was a riposte to AIDS activists who believed that their own mobilization against the "gay plague" had not only accelerated the science but bent the arc of political history toward emancipation. President Ronald Reagan initially ignored the AIDS outbreaks among gay men, Haitians, and hemophiliacs, and was deaf to the demands of AIDS Coalition to Unleash Power, whose acronym ACT UP reflected its methods. Finally, his surgeon general, C. Everett Koop, a fully credentialed conservative, and Anthony Fauci, just appointed to the job that he holds today, convinced Reagan to act.

The country's HIV and AIDS policies, and subsequently global policies too, were unprecedented in the history of public health responses to an incurable, sexually-transmitted disease targeting stigmatized groups—the designation of hemophiliacs and children born with HIV as "innocent victims" was the exception that proved that initial rule. People living with HIV and AIDS became involved in medical trials and policymaking. Activists offered to trial new drugs, arguing that they had nothing to lose by shortcutting the usual safety testing. They insisted on voluntary and confidential testing to protect their rights. In Africa government responses often ceded the agenda to civil society organizations and invariably included them in planning, and the international agencies set up to respond—UN-AIDS and the Global Fund to Fight HIV/AIDS, Tuberculosis and Malaria—pioneered a model of global health governance based on human rights and inclusion.

Why Epidemiologists Should Think Like Communities

I HAD A WALK-ON ROLE late in the HIV and AIDS drama, in collaborative research on the politics, security, and social aspects of the pandemic. And, writing in the spirit of Virchow, I insisted that there can *only* be a democratic public health. Like many others, I was inspired by physician and medical anthropologist Paul Farmer; his book *Infections and Inequalities* (1999) is a manifesto for a partnership between social medicine and radical politics. The associations between poverty, inequality, ill health, and exposure to epidemics are well established and do not need to be emphasized here. Conscious of Aylward's warning not to apply the "lesson" of the last epidemic to this one, I will make just one cautious, epidemiological point: there is in fact intriguing evidence that "people's science" can play a crucial role in blunting epidemics and ensuring they do not recur.

This is not to say we should romanticize folk medical wisdom: we shouldn't. People's epidemiology has more than its share of superstitions: numerous practices that are at best harmless and at worst dangerous or even fatal. Still, decades of people's experimentation and observation have generated some real scientific breakthroughs, the emblematic example of which is smallpox variolation. An enslaved African American known to history only as Onesimus, familiar with the widespread African practice of injecting tissue from the pustules of smallpox patients into healthy individuals to produce a much less virulent version of the disease, introduced variolation to Massachusetts settlers in the early eighteenth century. Its efficacy was so convincing that George Washington inoculated his soldiers en masse. In 1798 the procedure was adapted by English physician Edward Jenner in the form of cowpox variolation, which he named vaccination.

There is also a demonstrable recent record of people's science hastening the end of an epidemic. The case in point is Ebola in West Africa in 2014. Epidemiological models, which accurately charted the early, exponential growth phase of the epidemic, failed to predict its rapid decline. The models projected only burnout or a long taper as public health responses slowly reduced transmission, and not the remarkably rapid decrease that actually occurred. In *Ebola: How a People's Science Helped End an Epidemic* (2016), social anthropologist Paul Richards argues that the deficiency in the modeling is best explained by changes in intimate social behavior that could neither be captured by models nor even fully explained by people who were themselves altering the critical risk behaviors.

Anthropologists themselves did not connect the dots at the early stage of the outbreak. They had researched funerals and funeral rituals, but not the real danger point for contagion, which was the preparation of the body for burial. Family care for the sick was the other main context of transmission. Community health workers, social anthropologists, and epidemiologists had to speak to one another, understand each other's knowledge, and find ways of communicating it. As Richards shows, the communities quickly learned to think like epidemiologists and adapted new safer body-handling practices, and the official top-down policies followed afterward. Post hoc modeling of the epidemic trajectory confirms that the best simulation of the decline is based on the widespread adoption of a community-based strategy for screening and travel restriction, which has the advantage that it requires a 50 percent compliance rate to be effective. The author of the review concludes, "We know of no other similarly validated explanation for the end of the outbreak."

Each pandemic is different, but the logic of political action is much the same. Where political interests align with scientific advice, that advice becomes policy. This is where we can legitimately learn lessons. In the case of 1918, the lesson learned by world leaders gathering to found the League of Nations was that international health is a problem that demands international cooperation. Smallpox was eradicated by exactly this sort of multilateral initiative in the 1970s. Measles, like smallpox, is caused by a virus that has only human hosts and so too could be eradicated, but to the wealthy nations that funded international health programs, it was regarded as a harmless rite of passage for young children, even though it killed millions of them in poor countries every year. Because funds and political backing were available, the UN targeted polio instead: also a devastating disease but one far harder to eradicate, because the virus can exist in the wild.

In the case of HIV and AIDS, what "worked" was that pressure compelled governments to acknowledge their epidemic and respond, and public clamor forced pharmaceutical companies to bring down the cost of antiretroviral drugs so that treatment regimes at scale did not bankrupt African governments. Less unequivocally helpful was the pressure for strictly voluntary testing, which was codified as international best practice, even though compulsory or routine tests—in which the patient must specifically request *not* to be tested—could have helped prevent infections. And, as with any complex institution, political incentives came to align with the interests of the institution, sometimes at the expense of the problem to be solved. The result was that the UN pushed for similar policies and metrics for every country, even though each individual country's epidemic was different: some were centered on homosexual sex, others on heterosexual sex, yet others on intravenous drug use, and all had different social mores and networks. But it was simpler to standardize the package. In my book *AIDS and Power* (2006), I concluded that in African democracies, political incentives were structured to manage AIDS rather than to contain it: to provide treatment maximally and prevention barely sufficiently.

The 2003 SARS outbreak is the immediate precursor to COVID-19 in both pathogenesis and politics. It holds two political lessons. First, it shamed China's government, but not enough. The government concealed the initial outbreak and reacted too late—the coronavirus spread across the world sparking local outbreaks, notably in Canada. Commentators speculated that SARS could be the crisis that cracked the Communist Party's authoritarian control. In a volume reviewing the outbreak, Tony Saich asked whether SARS was "China's Chernobyl or Much Ado About Nothing?" Saich reserved judgment, concluding that the Chinese authorities *ought* to learn. And seventeen years on, Saich's assessment of the response to COVID-19 is "no, they didn't learn from the SARS epidemic." Implicit in this conclusion is that Premier Hu Jintao didn't pay a political price for his flawed response to the disease. China developed its medical laboratories but did not create incentives for health workers to become whistleblowers: the default option for low-level officials receiving bad news was to please their superiors by insisting that all was still well. Second, the speedy suppression of SARS removed the market for pharmacological products that could treat coronaviruses or inoculate against them. Capitalism has no incentive for preemptively responding to a future global public bad.

From this we distill the elementary and wholly unsurprising lesson that well-articulated political demands shape the politics of public health. Democracies can *demand* public health.

de Waal

In the next-to-last act of the Hamburg drama, Virchow ends the scene. He has already posed the key question—whether it was material interest, political ideology, or medical science that determined the outcome. And although none of the protagonists answered the question—neither the cholera vibrio, not von Pettenkofer and the city merchants and lawyers, not Koch and his emperor, and not even the dissonant chorus—Virchow makes the claim that social emancipation and democracy will finally overcome cholera.

Thinking Critically in a Pandemic

WHAT DOES ALL THIS MEAN for COVID-19? We face a new virus with uncertain epidemiology that threatens illness, death, and disruption on an enormous scale. Precisely because every commentator sees the pandemic through the lens of his or her preoccupations, it is exactly the right time to think critically, to place the pandemic in context, to pose questions.

The clearest questions are political. What should the public demand of its governments? Through hard-learned experience, AIDS policymakers developed a mantra: "know your epidemic, act on its politics." The motives for—and consequences of—public health measures have always gone far beyond controlling disease. Political interest trumps science—or, to be more precise, political interest legitimizes some scientific readings and not others. Pandemics are the occasion for political contests and history suggests that facts and logic are tools for combat, not arbiters of the outcome.

While public health officials urge the public to suspend normal activities to flatten the curve of viral transmission, political leaders also urge us to suspend our critique so that they can be one step ahead of the outcry when it comes. Rarely in recent history has the bureaucratic, obedience-inducing mode of governance of the "deep state" become so widely esteemed across the political spectrum. It is precisely at such a moment, when scientific rationality is honored, that we need to be most astutely aware of the political uses to which such expertise is put. Looking back to Hamburg in 1892, we can readily discern what was science and what was superstition. We need our critical faculties on high alert to make those distinctions today.

At the same time, COVID-19 has reminded a jaded and distrustful public how much our well-being—indeed our survival—depends upon astonishing advances in medical science and public health over the last 140 years. In an unmatched exercise of international collaboration, scientists are working across borders and setting aside professional rivalries and financial interests in pursuit of treatment and a vaccine. People are also learning to value epidemiologists whose models are proving uncannily prescient.

But epidemiologists don't know everything. In the end it is mundane, intimate, and unmeasured human activities such as hand-washing and social distancing that can make the difference between an epidemic curve that overwhelms the hospital capacity of an industrialized nation and one that doesn't. Richards reminds us of the hopeful lesson from Ebola: "It is striking how rapidly communities learnt to think like epidemiologists, and epidemiologists to think like communities." It is this joint learning—mutual trust between experts and common people—that holds out the best hope for controlling COVID-19. We should not assume a too simple tradeoff between security and liberty, but rather subject the response to vigorous democratic scrutiny and oversight—not just because we believe in justice, transparency, and accountability, but also because that demonstrably works for public health.

As we do so, it is imperative we attend to the language and metaphors that shape our thinking. Scientists absorb (fundamental) uncertainty within (measurable) risk; public discourse runs along channels carved by more than a century of military models for infectious disease control. By a kind of zoonosis from metaphor to policy, "fighting" coronavirus may, in the worst case, bring troops onto our streets and security surveillance into our personal lives. Minor acts of corporate charity, trumpeted at a White House bully pulpit, may falsely appear more significant than the solidarities of underpaid, overworked health workers who knowingly run risks every day. Other, democratic responses are necessary and possible: we need to think and talk them into being.

Perhaps the most difficult paradigm to shift will be to consider infectious agents not as aliens but as part of us—our DNA, microbiomes, and the ecologies that we are transforming in the Anthropocene. Our public discourses fail to appreciate how deeply pathogenic evolution is entangled in our disruption of the planet's ecosystem. We have known for decades that a single zoonotic infection could easily become pandemic, and that social institutions for epidemic control are essential to provide breathing space for medical science to play catch-up. Our political–economic system failed to create the material incentives and the popular narrative for this kind of global safety net—the same failure that has generated climate crisis.

This is the final, unfinished act of the drama. Can human beings find a way to treat the pathogen, not as an aberration, but as a reminder that we are fated to coexist in an unstable Anthropocene? To expand on the words of Margaret Chan, WHO director at the time of SARS, "The virus writes the rules"—there is no singular set of rules. We have collectively changed the rules of our ecosystems, and pathogens have surprised us with their nimble adaptations to a world that we believed was ours.

TECHNOCRACY AFTER COVID-19
Jonathan White

APRIL 27, 2020

"COVID-19 REPRESENTS A NEW FORM of economic shock that cannot be tackled using the textbooks of the past." So recently observed Christine Lagarde, head of the European Central Bank (ECB). That emergencies throw orthodoxies in the air seems clear; fresh problems demand fresh thinking. But her words also hint at how technocrats define themselves in a crisis. As much as these are the conditions in which expertise is challenged, they are also times of opportunity. Officials can recast themselves as practical, flexible, and independent-minded—possessors of the deeper insight that lies in knowing when to set aside yesterday's formulas. Crisis encourages the transformation of technocracy—and with it, the relation to politics.

Twentieth-century history shows how turbulent times can produce calls for expert-led government. Movements for technocracy emerged in the United States and Europe in the 1930s in response to the Great Depression, taking inspiration from the rationalism attributed to wartime planning. The kind of expertise they prized was marked by the experience of crisis. Practical in spirit, it was about knowing what works, and how to fix things when they break. Many consciously celebrated the figure of the engineer. In the United States, the writings of Thorstein Veblen, Howard Scott, and Walter Rautenstrauch likened society to a machine, calling for government as "social engineering."

More soberly and influentially, the engineer's outlook was present in Keynesian economics, emerging with the *General Theory* in 1936 as the basis of postwar technocracy. Formed in the encounter with mass unemployment, this was macroeconomics as problem solving. In a world assumed to be volatile and swayed by the "animal spirits," markets never quite worked as they should. The policymaker's role was to tinker and probe, to keep things working despite stresses, strains, and shocks. Confronted with a complex and changing reality, discretion and judgment were needed, along with the prudence to build in spare capacity for the unexpected.

As the Keynesian consensus passed with the energy crises of the 1970s, a new vision of technocracy emerged, based instead on the ideal of the *scientist*. For monetarists like Milton Friedman, previous orthodoxy rested on dubious propositions that needed rigorous testing: the economist-engineers had taken too much for granted. More than earlier liberals like Friedrich Hayek (himself a critic of "scientism"), *neo*liberals developed their ideas on the model of physics. Assuming basic stability in how the world works—how markets operate, why firms behave as they do—the economist-scientist was to seek general laws of causality, while technocracy was to use standard templates rather than personal judgment and discretion. Both would be a kind of anonymous process, politically invisible and independent. Central banking would be based, ideally, on fixed rules and delegated objectives (e.g. low inflation), while the International Monetary Fund (IMF) and World Bank would develop a Washington Consensus of standardized policies, for which post-communist societies were a convenient laboratory. There was a utopian current in this model of technocracy: rather than manage an imperfect order, the goal was the optimal arrangement.

But what about when things go wrong? Technocracy-as-science suits stable times, when the real world can passably resemble the laboratory. Emergencies disrupt this norm, since actions must be taken quickly, before all the evidence is in. When the Asian financial crisis hit in 1997, a different expertise seemed called for—know-how more than know-that, plus knowing what not to do. Enter the figure of the *doctor*, and a tendency to liken the newly globalized and financialized economy to an organism struck by pathogens. Faced with "Asian flu," the role of IMF policymakers was to tackle contagion. On the model of disease control, this approach recognized the reality of degenerative tendencies, while implying most were external to policy itself and not something for which officials were responsible. It also managed expectations. The doctor assumes change and decay. There was now no such thing as a perfect market order: sickness was always possible (implying, of course, that the system was healthy much of the time). In this increasingly uncertain world, the policymaker was licensed to make discretionary interventions and acquired the added role of offering "reassurance" to keep anxieties in check.

In the economic crises of the 2010s, and now most recently with COVID-19, problem solving is more than ever the name of the game.

A doctor's judgment lies in connecting case to known remedy, but this gets harder the more unfamiliar the disease. Today's economic technocracy is about using all tools in the toolkit—in that sense we are witnessing the return of the engineer. Decision-makers emphasize the need for ingenuity, discretion, and invention, from Mario Draghi's *"whatever it takes* to preserve the euro" to Lagarde's "everything necessary." Eurozone policy rules are re-described as "self-imposed limits," revisable to preserve deeper goals of stability. Nobel Prize–winning economists ask us to think of their discipline as "plumbing"—engineering at the sharp end where things can get messy. There is even a note of the theatrical in today's technocracy: like a good stage performer, Lagarde keeps suspense about measures to come, "because the impact will also be linked to the element of surprise."

If economic technocracy after COVID-19 continues to move in this direction, there are some reasons to be optimistic. After decades of an outlook based on general propositions about how markets supposedly function, a perspective more conscious of market failure—and sometimes the need to slow down the machine—sounds attractive. Whereas scientific expertise can be excessively specialized, here there is the promise of a more rounded perspective. Greater sensitivity to the particularities of implementation offers a vantage point from which to accept crosscutting claims to social justice. And when it is recognized that the system is only as good as the policies designed into it, accountability has a better foundation. While similar things might have been said a decade ago, the effects of COVID-19 may be more profound than those of 2008, occurring as they do against the backdrop of an existing crisis of Western capitalism.

But there are also notable grounds for caution. There is no reason to suppose crisis technocracy will serve left-wing, even Keynesian, objectives: a willingness to intervene in the face of shocks can serve any number of ends. Moreover, crisis management only blurs ever more the boundary between technocracy and politics. As personal discretion comes to the fore, the notion that technocrats are just enacting a set of delegated tasks becomes untenable—their power is more elastic. One might even question how much expertise is actually present. Scientific knowledge is anchored in replicable methods, but know-how is harder to objectify. More personalized and intuitive, invoked when things are already going wrong, it can be hard to distinguish from arbitrary rule. How do we know who has it? Should this authority not be contested?

When officials distance themselves from "the textbooks of the past," they redefine their expertise and embrace the flexibility sought in extreme conditions. Crisis decisions may be better for it. But as technocrats go down this path, one may question whether technocracy remains the right standard to apply.

HOW EPIDEMICS END

Jeremy A. Greene & Dóra Vargha

JUNE 30, 2020

RECENT HISTORY TELLS US A LOT about how epidemics unfold, how outbreaks spread, and how they are controlled. We also know a good deal about beginnings—those first cases of pneumonia in Guangdong marking the SARS outbreak of 2002–3, the earliest instances of influenza in Veracruz leading to the H1N1 influenza pandemic of 2009–10, the outbreak of hemorrhagic fever in Guinea sparking the Ebola pandemic of 2014–16. But these stories of rising action and a dramatic denouement only get us so far in coming to terms with the global crisis of COVID-19. The coronavirus pandemic has blown past many efforts at containment, snapped the reins of case detection and surveillance across the world, and saturated all inhabited continents. To understand possible endings for this epidemic, we must look elsewhere than the neat pattern of beginning and end—and reconsider what we mean by the talk of "ending" epidemics to begin with.

Historians have long been fascinated by epidemics in part because, even where they differ in details, they exhibit a typical pattern of social choreography recognizable across vast reaches of time and space. Even though the biological agents of the sixth-century Plague of Justinian, the fourteenth-century Black Death, and the early twentieth-century Manchurian Plague were almost certainly not identical, the epidemics themselves share common features that link historical actors to present experience. "As a social phenomenon," historian Charles Rosenberg has argued, "an epidemic has a dramaturgic form. Epidemics start at a moment in time, proceed on a stage limited in space and duration, following a plot line of increasing and revelatory tension, move to a crisis of individual and collective character, then drift towards closure." And yet not all diseases fit so neatly into this typological structure. Rosenberg wrote these words in 1989, nearly a decade into the North American HIV/AIDS epidemic. His words rang true about the origins of that disease—thanks in part to the relentless, overzealous pursuit of its "Patient Zero"—but not so much about its end, which was, as for COVID-19, nowhere in sight.

In the case of the new coronavirus, we have now seen an initial fixation on origins give way to the question of endings. In March the *Atlantic* offered four possible "timelines for life returning to normal," all of which depended on the biological basis of a sufficient amount of the population developing immunity (perhaps 60 to 80 percent) to curb further spread. This confident assertion derived from models of infectious outbreaks formalized by epidemiologists such as W. H. Frost a century earlier. If the world can be defined into those susceptible (S), infected (I) and resistant (R) to a disease, and a pathogen has a reproductive number R_0 (pronounced R-naught) describing how many susceptible people can be infected by a single infected person, the end of the epidemic begins when the proportion of susceptible people drops below the reciprocal, $1/R_0$. When that happens, one person would infect, on average, less than one other person with the disease.

These formulas reassure us, perhaps deceptively. They conjure up a set of natural laws that give order to the cadence of calamities. The curves produced by models, which in better times belonged to the arcana of epidemiologists, are now common figures in the lives of billions of people learning to live with contractions of civil society promoted in the name of "bending," "flattening," or "squashing" them. At the same time, the smooth lines of these curves are far removed from jagged realities of the day-to-day experience of an epidemic—including the sharp spikes in those "reopening" states where modelers had predicted continued decline.

In other words, epidemics are not merely biological phenomena. They are inevitably framed and shaped by our social responses to them, from beginning to end (whatever the end may mean in any particular case). The questions now being asked of scientists, clinicians, mayors, governors, prime ministers, and presidents around the world is not merely "When will the biological phenomenon of this epidemic resolve?" but rather "When, if ever, will the disruption to our social life caused in the name of coronavirus come to an end?" As peak incidence nears, and in many places appears to have passed, elected officials and think tanks from opposite ends of the political spectrum provide "roadmaps" and "frameworks" for how an epidemic that has shut down economic, civic, and social life in a manner not seen globally in at least a century might eventually recede and allow resumption of a "new normal."

Greene & Vargha

These two faces of an epidemic, the biological and the social, are closely intertwined, but they are not the same. The biological epidemic can shut down daily life by sickening and killing people, but the social epidemic also shuts down daily life by overturning basic premises of sociality, economics, governance, discourse, interaction—and killing people in the process as well. There is a risk, as we know from both the influenza of 1918–19 and the more recent swine flu of 2008–9, of relaxing social responses before the biological threat has passed. But there is also a risk in misjudging a biological threat based on faulty models or bad data and in disrupting social life in such a way that the restrictions can never properly be taken back. We have seen the two faces of the coronavirus epidemic escalating in tandem, but the biological epidemic and the social epidemic don't necessarily recede on the same timeline.

For these sorts of reasons, we must step back and reflect in detail on what we mean by ending in the first place. The history of epidemic endings has taken many forms, and only a handful of them have resulted in the elimination of a disease.

HISTORY REMINDS US that the interconnections between the timing of the biological and social epidemics are far from obvious. In some cases, like the yellow fever epidemics of the eighteenth century and the cholera epidemics of the nineteenth century, the dramatic symptomatology of the disease itself can make its timing easy to track. Like a bag of popcorn popping in the microwave, the tempo of visible case-events begins slowly, escalates to a frenetic peak, and then recedes, leaving a diminishing frequency of new cases that eventually are spaced far enough apart to be contained and then eliminated. In other examples, however, like the polio epidemics of the twentieth century, the disease process itself is hidden, often mild in presentation, threatens to come back, and ends not on a single day but over different timescales and in different ways for different people.

Campaigns against infectious diseases are often discussed in military terms, and one result of that metaphor is to suggest that epidemics too must have a singular endpoint. We approach the infection peak as if it were a decisive battle like Waterloo, or a diplomatic arrangement like the Armistice at Compiègne in November 1918. Yet the chronology of a single, decisive ending is not always true even for military history, of course. Just as the clear ending of a military war does not necessarily bring a close to the experience of war in everyday life, so too the resolution of the biological epidemic does not immediately undo the effects of the social epidemic. The social and economic effects of the 1918–19 pandemic, for example, were felt long after the end of the third and putatively final wave of the virus. While the immediate economic effect on many local businesses caused by shutdowns appears to have resolved in a matter of months, the broader economic effects of the epidemic on labor-wage relations were still visible in economic surveys in 1920, again in 1921, and in several areas as far as 1930.

And yet, like World War I with which its history was so closely intertwined, the influenza pandemic of 1918–19 appeared at first to have a singular ending. In individual cities, the epidemic often produced dramatic spikes and falls in equally rapid tempo. In Philadelphia, as John Barry notes in *The Great Influenza* (2004), after an explosive and deadly rise in October 1919 that peaked at 4,597 deaths in a single week, cases suddenly dropped so precipitously that the public gathering ban could be lifted before the month was over, with almost no new cases in the following weeks. A phenomenon whose destructive potential was limited by material laws, "the virus burned through available fuel, then it quickly faded away."

As Barry reminds us, however, scholars have since learned to differentiate at least three different sequences of epidemics within the broader pandemic. The first wave blazed through military installations in the spring of 1918, the second wave caused the devastating mortality spikes in the summer and fall of 1918, and the third wave began in December 1918 and lingered long through the summer of 1919. Some cities, like San Francisco, passed through the first and second waves relatively unscathed only to be devastated by the third wave. Nor was it clear to those still alive in 1919 that the pandemic was over after the third wave receded. Even as late as 1922, a bad flu season in Washington State merited a response from public health officials to enforce absolute quarantine as they had during 1918–19. It is difficult, looking back, to say exactly when this prototypical pandemic of the twentieth century was really over.

WHO CAN TELL when a pandemic has ended? Today, strictly speaking, only the World Health Organization (WHO). The Emergency

Committee of the WHO is responsible for the global governance of health and international coordination of epidemic response. After the SARS coronavirus pandemic of 2002–3, this body was granted sole power to declare the beginnings and endings of Public Health Emergencies of International Concern (PHEIC). While SARS morbidity and mortality—roughly 8,000 cases and 800 deaths in 26 countries—has been dwarfed by the sheer scale of COVID-19, the pandemic's effect on national and global economies prompted revisions to the International Health Regulations in 2005, a body of international law that had remained unchanged since 1969. This revision broadened the scope of coordinated global response from a handful of diseases to any public health event that the WHO deemed to be of international concern. It also shifted from a reactive response framework to a proactive one based on real-time surveillance and from action at borders to detection and containment at the source.

This social infrastructure has important consequences, not all of them necessarily positive. Any time the WHO declares a public health event of international concern—and frequently when it chooses *not* to declare one—the event becomes a matter of front-page news. Since the 2005 revision, the group has been criticized both for declaring a PHEIC too hastily (as in the case of H1N1) or too late (in the case of Ebola). The WHO's decision to declare the *end* of a PHEIC, by contrast, is rarely subject to the same public scrutiny. When an outbreak is no longer classified as an "extraordinary event" and no longer is seen to pose a risk at international spread, the PHEIC is considered not to be justified, leading to a withdrawal of international coordination. Once countries can grapple with the disease within their own borders, under their own national frameworks, the PHEIC is quietly de-escalated.

As the response to the 2014–16 Ebola outbreak in West Africa demonstrates, however, the act of declaring the end of a pandemic can be just as powerful as the act of declaring its beginning—in part because emergency situations can continue even after a return to "normal" has been declared. When WHO director general Margaret Chan announced in March 2016 that the Ebola outbreak was no longer a public health event of international concern, international donors withdrew funds and care to the West African countries devastated by the outbreak, even as these struggling health systems continued to be stretched beyond their means by the needs of Ebola survivors. NGOs and virologists expressed concern that efforts to fund Ebola vaccine development would likewise fade without a sense of global urgency pushing research forward.

Part of the reason that the role of the WHO in proclaiming and terminating the state of pandemic is subject to so much scrutiny is that it *can* be. The WHO is the only global health body that is accountable to all governments of the world; its parliamentary World Health Assembly contains health ministers from every nation. Its authority rests not so much on its battered budget as its access to epidemic intelligence and pool of select individuals, technical experts with vast experience in epidemic response. But even though internationally sourced scientific and public health authority is key to its role in pandemic crises, WHO guidance is ultimately carried out in very different ways and on very different time scales in different countries, provinces, states, counties, and cities. One state might begin to ease up restrictions to movement and industry just as another implements more and more stringent measures. If each country's experience of "lockdown" has already been heterogeneous, the reconnection between them after the PHEIC is ended will likely show even more variance.

SO MANY OF OUR HOPES for the termination of the present PHEIC now lie in the promise of a COVID-19 vaccine. Yet a closer look at one of the central vaccine success stories of the twentieth century shows that technological solutions rarely offer resolution to pandemics on their own. Contrary to our expectations, vaccines are not universal technologies. They are always deployed locally, with variable resources and commitments to scientific expertise. International variations in research, development, and dissemination of effective vaccines are especially relevant in the global fight against epidemic polio.

The development of the polio vaccine is relatively well known, usually told as a story of a U.S. tragedy and triumph. Yet while polio epidemics that swept the globe in the postwar decades did not respect national borders or the Iron Curtain, the Cold War provided context for both collaboration and antagonism. Only a few years after the licensing of Jonas Salk's inactivated vaccine in the United States, his technique became widely used across the world, although its efficacy outside of the United States was questioned. The second, live oral vaccine developed by Albert Sabin, however, involved extensive collaboration with Eastern European and Soviet colleagues. As the success of the Soviet polio vaccine trials marked a rare landmark of Cold War cooperation, Basil O'Connor, president of the March of Dimes movement, speaking at the Fifth International Poliomyelitis Conference in 1960, proclaimed that "in search for the truth that frees man from disease, there is no cold war."

Yet the differential uptake of this vaccine retraced the divisions of Cold War geography. The Soviet Union, Hungary, and Czechoslovakia were the first countries in the world to begin nationwide immunization with the Sabin vaccine, soon followed by Cuba, the first country in the Western Hemisphere to eliminate the disease. By the time the Sabin vaccine was licensed in the United States in 1963, much of Eastern Europe had done away with epidemics and was largely polio-free. The successful ending of this epidemic within the communist world was immediately held up as proof of the superiority of that political system.

Western experts who trusted the Soviet vaccine trials, including Yale virologist and WHO envoy Dorothy Horstmann, nonetheless emphasized that their results were possible because of the military-like organization of the Soviet health care system. Yet these enduring concerns that authoritarianism itself was the key tool for ending epidemics—a concern reflected in current debates over China's heavy-handed interventions in Wuhan this year—can also be overstated. The Cold War East was united not only by authoritarianism and heavy hierarchies in state organization and society, but also by a powerful shared belief in the integration of paternal state, biomedical research, and socialized medicine. Epidemic management in these countries combined an emphasis on prevention, easily mobilized health workers, top-down organization of vaccinations, and a rhetoric of solidarity, all resting on a health care system that aimed at access to all citizens.

Still, authoritarianism as a catalyst for controlling epidemics can be singled out and pursued with long-lasting consequences. Epidemics can be harbingers of significant political changes that go well beyond their ending, significantly reshaping a new "normal" after the threat passes. Many Hungarians, for example, have watched with alarm the complete sidelining of parliament and the introduction of government by decree at the end of March this year. The end of any epidemic crisis, and thus the end of the need for the significantly increased power of Viktor Orbán, would be determined by Orbán himself. Likewise, many other states, urging the mobilization of new technologies as a solution to end epidemics, are opening the door to heightened state surveillance of their citizens. The apps and trackers now being designed to follow the movement and exposure of people in order to enable the end of epidemic lockdowns can collect data and establish mechanisms that reach well beyond the original intent. The digital afterlives of these practices raise new and unprecedented questions about when and how epidemics end.

Although we want to believe that a single technological break-through will end the present crisis, the application of any global health technology is always locally determined. After its dramatic successes in managing polio epidemics in the late 1950s and early 1960s, the oral poliovirus vaccine became the tool of choice for the Global Polio Eradication Initiative in the late 1980s, as it promised an end to "summer fears" globally. But since vaccines are in part technologies of trust, ending polio outbreaks depends on maintaining confidence in national and international structures through which vaccines are delivered. Wherever that often fragile trust is fractured or undermined, vaccination rates can drop to a critical level, giving way to vaccine-derived polio, which thrives in partially vaccinated populations.

In Kano, Nigeria, for example, a ban on polio vaccination between 2000 and 2004 resulted in a new national polio epidemic that soon spread to neighboring countries. As late as December 2019 polio outbreaks were still reported in fifteen African countries, including Angola and the Democratic Republic of the Congo. Nor is it clear that polio can fully be regarded as an epidemic at this point: while polio epidemics are now a thing of the past for Hungary—and the rest of Europe, the Americas, Australia, and East Asia as well—the disease is still endemic to parts of Africa and South Asia. A disease once universally epidemic is now locally endemic: this, too, is another way that epidemics end.

INDEED, many epidemics have only "ended" through widespread acceptance of a newly endemic state. Consider the global threat of HIV/AIDS. From a strictly biological perspective, the AIDS epidemic has never ended; the virus continues to spread devastation through the world, infecting 1.7 million people and claiming an estimated 770,000 lives in 2018 alone. But HIV is not generally described these days with the same urgency and fear that accompanied the newly defined

AIDS epidemic in the early 1980s. Like coronavirus today, AIDS at that time was a rapidly spreading and unknown emerging threat, splayed across newspaper headlines and magazine covers, claiming the lives of celebrities and ordinary citizens alike. Nearly forty years later, it has largely become a chronic disease endemic, at least in the Global North. Like diabetes, which claimed an estimated 4.9 million lives in 2019, HIV/AIDS became a manageable condition—if one had access to the right medications.

Those who are no longer directly threatened by the impact of the disease have a hard time continuing to attend to the urgency of an epidemic that has been rolling on for nearly four decades. Even in the first decade of the AIDS epidemic, activists in the United States fought tooth and nail to make their suffering visible in the face of both the Reagan administration's dogged refusal to talk publicly about the AIDS crisis and the indifference of the press after the initial sensation of the newly discovered virus had become common knowledge. In this respect, the social epidemic does not necessarily end when biological transmission has ended, or even peaked, but rather when, in the attention of the general public and in the judgment of certain media and political elites who shape that attention, the disease ceases to be newsworthy.

Polio, for its part, has not been newsworthy for a while, even as thousands around the world still live with polio with ever-decreasing access to care and support. Soon after the immediate threat of outbreaks passed, so did support for those whose lives were still bound up with the disease. For others, it became simply a background fact of life—something that happens elsewhere. The polio problem was "solved," specialized hospitals were closed, fundraising organizations found new causes, and poster children found themselves in an increasingly challenging world. Few medical professionals are trained today in the treatment of the disease. As intimate knowledge of polio and its treatment withered away with time, people living with polio became embodied repositories of lost knowledge.

History tells us public attention is much more easily drawn to new diseases as they emerge rather than sustained over the long haul. Well before AIDS shocked the world into recognizing the devastating potential of novel epidemic diseases, a series of earlier outbreaks had already signaled the presence of emerging infectious agents. When hundreds of members of the American Legion fell ill after their annual meeting in Philadelphia in 1976, the efforts of epidemiologists from the Centers for Disease Control to explain the spread of this mysterious disease and its newly discovered bacterial agent, *Legionella*, occupied front-page headlines. In the years since, however, as the 1976 incident faded from memory, Legionella infections have become everyday objects of medical care, even though incidence in the United States has grown ninefold since 2000, tracing a line of exponential growth that looks a lot like COVID-19's on a longer time scale. Yet few among us pause in our daily lives to consider whether we are living through the slowly ascending limb of a Legionella epidemic.

Nor do most people living in the United States stop to consider the ravages of tuberculosis as a pandemic, even though an estimated 10 million new cases of tuberculosis were reported around the globe in 2018, and an estimated 1.5 million people died from the disease. The disease seems to only receive attention in relation to newer scourges: in the late twentieth century, TB coinfection became a leading cause of death in emerging HIV/AIDS pandemic, while in the past few months it has been invoked as a rising cause of mortality in COVID-19 pandemic. Amidst these stories it is easy to miss that on its own, tuberculosis has been, and continues to be, the leading cause of death worldwide from a single infectious agent. And even though tuberculosis is not an active concern of middle-class Americans, it is still not a thing of the past even in this country. More than 9,000 cases of tuberculosis were reported in the United States in 2018—overwhelmingly affecting racial and ethnic minority populations—but they rarely made the news.

While tuberculosis is the target of concerted international disease control efforts, and occasionally eradication efforts, the time course of this affliction has been spread out so long—and so clearly demarcated in space as a problem of "other places"—that it is no longer part of the epidemic imagination of the Global North. And yet history tells a very different story. DNA lineage studies of tuberculosis now show that the spread of tuberculosis in sub-Saharan Africa and Latin America was initiated by European contact and conquest from the fifteenth century through the nineteenth. In the early decades of the twentieth century, tuberculosis epidemics accelerated throughout sub-Saharan Africa, South Asia, and Southeast Asia due to the rapid urbanization and industrialization of European colonies. Although the wave of decolonizations that swept these regions between the 1940s and the 1980s established autonomy and sovereignty for newly postcolonial nations, this movement did not send tuberculosis back to Europe.

These features of the social lives of epidemics—how they live on even when they seem, to some, to have disappeared—show them to be not just natural phenomena but also narrative ones: deeply shaped by the stories we tell about their beginnings, their middles, their ends. At their best, epidemic endings are a form of relief for the mainstream "we" that can pick up the pieces and reconstitute a normal life. At their worst, epidemic endings are a form of collective amnesia, transmuting the disease that remains into merely someone else's problem.

WHAT ARE WE TO CONCLUDE from these complex interactions between the social and the biological faces of epidemics, past and present? Like infectious agents on an agar plate, epidemics colonize our social lives and force us to learn to live with them, in some way or another, for the foreseeable future. Just as the postcolonial period continued to be shaped by structures established under colonial rule, so too are our post-pandemic futures indelibly shaped by what we do now. There will be no simple return to the way things were: whatever normal we build will be a new one—whether many of us realize it or not. Like the world of scientific facts after the end of a critical experiment, the world that we find after the end of an epidemic crisis—whatever we take that to be—looks in many ways like the world that came before, but with new social truths established. How exactly these norms come into being depends a great deal on particular circumstances: current interactions among people, the instruments of social policy as well as medical and public health intervention with which we apply our efforts, and the underlying response of the material which we applied that apparatus against (in this case, the coronavirus strain SARS-CoV-2). While we cannot know now how the present epidemic will end, we can be confident that it in its wake it will leave different conceptions of normal in realms biological and social, national and international, economic and political.

Though we like to think of science as universal and objective, crossing borders and transcending differences, it is in fact deeply contingent upon local practices—including norms that are easily thrown over in an emergency, and established conventions that do not always hold up in situations of urgency. Today we see civic leaders jumping the gun in speaking of access to treatments, antibody screens, and vaccines well in advance of any scientific evidence, while relatively straightforward attempts to estimate the true number of people affected by the disease spark firestorms over the credibility of medical knowledge. Arduous work is often required to achieve scientific consensus, and when the stakes are high—especially when huge numbers of lives are at risk—heterogeneous data give way to highly variable interpretations. As data moves too quickly in some domains and too slowly in others, and sped-up time pressures are placed on all investigations, the projected curve of the epidemic is transformed into an elaborate guessing game, in which different states rely on different kinds of scientific claims to sketch out wildly different timetables for ending social restrictions.

These varied endings of the epidemic across local and national settings will only be valid insofar as they are acknowledged as such by others—especially if any reopening of trade and travel is to be achieved. In this sense, the process of establishing a new normal in global commerce will continue to be bound up in practices of international consensus. What the new normal in global health governance will look like, however, is more uncertain than ever. Long accustomed to the role of international scapegoat, the WHO secretariat seems doomed to be accused either of working beyond its mandate or not acting fast enough. Moreover, it can easily become a target of scapegoating, as the secessionist posturing of Donald Trump demonstrates. Yet the U.S. president's recent withdrawal from this international body is neither unprecedented nor unsurmountable. Although Trump's voting base might not wish to be grouped together with the only other global power to secede from the WHO, after the Soviet Union's 1949 departure from the group it ultimately brought all Eastern Bloc back to task of international health leadership in 1956. Much as the return of the Soviets to the WHO resulted in the global eradication of smallpox—the only human disease so far to have been intentionally eradicated—it is possible that some future return of the United States to the project of global health governance might also result in a more hopeful post-pandemic future.

As historians at the University of Oslo have recently noted, in epidemic periods "the present moves faster, the past seems further removed, and the future seems completely unpredictable." How, then, are we to know when epidemics end? How does the act of looking back aid us in determining a way forward? Historians make poor futurologists, but we spend a lot of time thinking about time. And epidemics produce their own kinds of time, in both biological and social domains, disrupting our individual senses of passing days as well as conventions for collective behavior. They carry within them their own tempo and rhythm: the slow initial growth, the explosive upward limb of the outbreak, the slowing of transmission that marks the peak, plateau, and the downward limb. This falling action is perhaps best thought of as asymptotic: rarely disappearing, but rather fading to the point where signal is lost in the noise of the new normal—and even allowed to be forgotten.

PANDEMIC PHILOSOPHY

Science & Action Under Uncertainty

MODELS VERSUS EVIDENCE
Jonathan Fuller

MAY 5, 2020

THE LASTING ICON OF THE COVID-19 PANDEMIC will likely be the graphic associated with "flattening the curve." The image is now familiar: a skewed bell curve measuring coronavirus cases that towers above a horizontal line—the health system's capacity—only to be flattened by an invisible force representing "non-pharmaceutical interventions" such as school closures, social distancing, and full-on lockdowns.

How do the coronavirus models generating these hypothetical curves square with the evidence? What roles do models and evidence play in a pandemic? Answering these questions requires reconciling two competing philosophies in the science of COVID-19.

In one camp are infectious disease epidemiologists, who work very closely with institutions of public health. They have used a multitude of models to create virtual worlds in which sim viruses wash over sim populations—sometimes unabated, sometimes held back by a virtual dam of social interventions. This deluge of simulated outcomes played a significant role in leading government actors to shut borders as well as doors to schools and businesses. But the hypothetical curves are smooth, while real-world data are rough. Some detractors have questioned whether we have good evidence for the assumptions the models rely on, and even the necessity of the dramatic steps taken to curb the pandemic. Among this camp are several clinical epidemiologists, who typically provide guidance for clinical practice—regarding, for example, the effectiveness of medical interventions—rather than public health.

The latter camp has won significant media attention in recent weeks. Bill Gates—whose foundation funds the research behind the most visible outbreak model in the United States, developed by the Institute for Health Metrics and Evaluation (IHME) at the University of Washington—worries that COVID-19 might be a "once-in-a-century pandemic." A notable detractor from this view is Stanford's John Ioannidis, a clinical epidemiologist, meta-researcher, and reliable skeptic who has openly wondered whether the coronavirus pandemic might rather be a "once-in-a-century evidence fiasco." He argues that better data are needed to justify the drastic measures undertaken to contain the pandemic in the United States and elsewhere.

Ioannidis claims, in particular, that our data about the pandemic are unreliable, leading to exaggerated estimates of risk. He also points to a systematic review published in 2011 of the evidence regarding physical interventions that aim to reduce the spread of respiratory viruses, worrying that the available evidence is nonrandomized and prone to bias. (A systematic review specific to COVID-19 has now been published; it concurs that the quality of evidence is "low" to "very low" but nonetheless supports the use of quarantine and other public health measures.) According to Ioannidis, the current steps we are taking are "non-evidence-based." This talk of "biased evidence" and "evidence-based interventions" is characteristic of the evidence-based medicine (EBM) community, a close relative of clinical epidemiology. In a series of blog posts, for example, Tom Jefferson and Carl Heneghan of the Oxford Centre for Evidence-Based Medicine similarly lament the poor-quality data and evidence guiding action in the pandemic and even suggest that lockdown is the wrong call.

In the other corner, Harvard's Marc Lipsitch, an infectious disease epidemiologist, agrees that we lack good data in many respects. Countering Ioannidis's hesitation, however, Lipsitch responds: "We know enough to act; indeed, there is an imperative to act strongly and swiftly." According to this argument, we could not afford to wait for better data when the consequences of delaying action are disastrous, and did have reason enough to act decisively.

Public health epidemiologists and clinical epidemiologists have overlapping methods and expertise; they all seek to improve health by studying populations. Yet to some extent, public health epidemiology and clinical epidemiology are distinct traditions in health care, competing philosophies of scientific knowledge. Public health epidemiology, including infectious disease epidemiology, tends to embrace theory and diversity of data; it is methodologically liberal and pragmatic. Clinical epidemiology, by contrast, tends to champion evidence and quality of data; it is comparatively more methodologically conservative and skeptical. (There is currently a movement in public health epidemiology that is in some ways closer to the clinical epidemiology philosophy, but I won't discuss it here.)

To be clear, these comparisons are fair only writ large; they describe disciplinary orthodoxy as a whole rather than the work of any given epidemiologist. Still, it is possible to discern two distinct philosophies in epidemiology, and both have something to offer in the coronavirus crisis over models and evidence. A deeper understanding of modeling and evidence is the key not only to reconciling these divergent scientific mindsets but also to resolving the crisis.

Models

PUBLIC HEALTH EPIDEMIOLOGY uses theory, especially theory from other health sciences such as microbiology, to model infection and understand patterns and causes of disease. Many of the epidemic models that the public and public health researchers alike have been voraciously consuming—including models produced by Imperial College London that informed the coronavirus response in both the United Kingdom and the United States—are SIR-type models. The theory underlying these models is old, originating in the Kermack–McKendrick theory in the 1920s and '30s, and even earlier in the germ theory in the second half of the nineteenth century. The SIR framework partitions a population into at least three groups: those who are susceptible to future infection (S), those who are currently infectious (I), and those who have been removed from the infectious group through recovery or death (R). An SIR model uses a system of differential equations to model the dynamics of the outbreak, the movement of individuals among the various groups over time.

Other models in the SIR family add additional groups to these three basic ones, such as a group for those who are infected with the virus but not yet infectious to others. Agent-based models also represent infection dynamics (how the number of cases changes over time), but they do so by modeling behaviors for each member of the simulated population individually. Curve-fitting models like the one used by the IHME are less theoretical; they extrapolate from previous infection curves to make predictions about the future. All these different models have been used in the COVID-19 pandemic. The diversity of approaches, along with divergent estimates for model parameters, partly explains the range of predictions we have seen.

Public health epidemiology also relies on a diversity of data—from multiple regions, using a variety of methods—to answer any one scientific question. In the coronavirus pandemic, in particular, research groups have used estimates of multiple key parameters of the outbreak (infection rate, average duration of illness) derived from multiple settings (China, Italy) and produced by various kinds of studies (population-based, laboratory-based, clinically based) to make projections. Public health epidemiology is liberal in the sense of relying on multiple tools, including modeling techniques (the Imperial College team has used several models), and also in the sense of simulating various possibilities by tweaking a model's assumptions. Finally, its philosophy is pragmatic. It embraces theory, diversity of data, and modeling as a means to reaching a satisfactory decision, often in circumstances where the evidence is far from definitive but time or practical constraints get in the way of acquiring better evidence.

A formative scientific moment for the public health epidemiology tradition was the epidemiological research on smoking and lung cancer in the 1950s and '60s. Although lung cancer is not an infectious disease and SIR modeling played no starring role in this research, it featured a similar scientific approach and philosophical outlook. The public health epidemiology philosophy is especially necessary early on in an outbreak of a novel pathogen, when untested assumptions greatly outnumber data, yet predictions and decisions must still be made.

Neil Ferguson, one of the leading epidemiologists behind the Imperial College models, describes epidemic modeling as "building simplified representations of reality." The characterization is apt because SIR-type models have variables and equations meant to represent real features of the populations modeled. (Other types of scientific tools, such as black box neural nets used in machine learning, work differently: they do not attempt to mirror the world but simply to predict its behavior.) We could therefore ask how well an SIR-type model mirrors reality. However, the primary use of the models, especially early on in an epidemic, is to predict the future of the outbreak, rather than to help us explain or understand it. As a result, the most important question we can ask of an outbreak model during a crisis is not whether its assumptions are accurate but instead how well it predicts the future—a hard-nosed practical question rather than a theoretical one.

Of course, predictive power is not totally unrelated to a model's representational accuracy. One way to improve the predictive prowess of a model is to go out and collect data that can confirm or deny the accuracy of its assumptions. But that's not the only way. By running many simulations of the same model under different assumptions (so-called sensitivity analysis), a modeler can determine how sensitive the model's predictions are to changes in its assumptions. By learning from multiple different models, a scientist can also triangulate, so to speak, on a more robust prediction that is less susceptible to the faults of any one model. Both strategies were used in determining UK coronavirus policy.

Finally, often a single, more accurate prediction based on high-quality evidence is less useful than a range of modeling predictions that capture best-case and worst-case scenarios (such as the range of death counts the White House coronavirus taskforce presented at the end of March). It might be prudent to plan for the worst case and not only the most likely possibility. A pragmatic philosophy generally serves public health decision makers well.

However, when certain predictions based on plausible model assumptions would lead decision-makers to radically different policy recommendations, the assumptions should be investigated with further evidence. A team at Oxford University, for example, performed epidemic modeling specifically to illustrate that worrying coronavirus projections depend crucially on estimates of the number of individuals previously infected and now immune to the virus. It is this kind of uncertainty that serves as fodder for the evidence thumpers.

Fuller

Evidence

CLINICAL EPIDEMIOLOGISTS are playing their own part in the pandemic: they are designing clinical trials of COVID-19 treatments, such as the multi-country Solidarity trial organized by the World Health Organization. In keeping with the high standards of evidence in the EBM movement, these trials are randomized: individuals are randomly allocated to receive one treatment or another (or a different combination of treatments). Although opinions on the exact virtues of randomization vary slightly, the most popular idea is that randomization reduces systematic bias. In a clinical trial, randomization eliminates selection bias, resulting in trial groups that are more representative or comparable in terms of causally relevant background features. Randomized studies are preferred because they can generate evidence that is less biased and more accurate.

The concept of evidence is central to clinical epidemiology and EBM alike. Clinical epidemiology research produces evidence, while EBM experts critically appraise it. Good evidence, this tradition says, consists mainly in the results of clinical epidemiology studies. The tradition is generally suspicious of theory, including reasoning based on pathophysiology and models of disease. It often cautions that theory can sometimes mislead us—for instance, by smuggling in unproven assumptions that have not been empirically established in human populations. In the coronavirus case, models assume—based on experience with other pathogens, but not concrete evidence with the new coronavirus—that individuals who recover from infection will develop immunity against reinfection, at least in the short term.

A central concern for this philosophy is not the diversity but the quality of data. A founding principle of EBM is that the best medical decisions are those that are based on the best available evidence, and evidence is better if it consists of higher-quality data. EBM provides guidance on which evidence is best, but clinical epidemiological methods such as meta-analysis do not allow one to amalgamate diverse kinds of evidence. The tradition is also conservative in basing conclusions only on well-established empirical results rather than speculative modeling, preferring "gold standard" randomized studies to hypothetical simulations. Finally, this tradition is skeptical, challenging assumptions, authority, and dogma, always in search of study design flaws and quick to point out the limitations of research.

A formative moment for the clinical epidemiology tradition was the British Medical Research Council's 1948 trial of streptomycin for tuberculosis, widely considered to be one of the first modern randomized clinical trials. This philosophy can be especially helpful as an outbreak of a novel pathogen evolves: over time better evidence becomes available to scrutinize previous assumptions and settle unanswered questions. Clinical epidemiology has the expertise to contribute much of this evidence.

In advocating for evidence-based public health measures, Ioannidis suggests subjecting interventions like social distancing measures to randomized trials. His suggestion may not be feasible in the United States given multiple levels of governance over social distancing policies, among other logistical difficulties. But the suggestion that we should be studying the effectiveness of our public health interventions is as important as it is obvious, and clinical epidemiology is well placed to contribute to this endeavor. While public health epidemiology is adept at studying the distributions and determinants of disease, clinical epidemiology is at home in studying the effectiveness of health care interventions. (I do not mean to suggest that public health epidemiology simply lacks the resources to study its own interventions. Imperial College London published a clever impact study, for example, of the interventions it recommended.)

Measuring the effects of public health measures is far from trivial. Social distancing is not an intervention: it is a mixed bag of individual behaviors, some voluntary and some involuntary. These behaviors are represented in outbreak models by simulating reduced social interactions. The models sometimes suppose that certain specific interventions, such as school or business closures, will produce particular patterns of social mixing. But the *effects* of specific interventions on patterns of social mixing is not the target of a classic SIR model. The modeler *inputs* patterns of social interaction; the model doesn't spit them out. (However, disease-behavior models *do* model social dynamics together with viral dynamics.) Rigorous research is needed to separate out the effects of individual interventions that have often been implemented simultaneously and are difficult to disentangle from independent behavior changes. Moreover, our interventions might have independent effects (on health, on the economy), and an outbreak model isn't broad enough in scope to predict these effects.

Ioannidis also suggests a solution to the problem of inaccurate pandemic statistics: testing representative population samples, rather than relying on samples subject to sampling bias. In order to estimate the number of infected people and the growth of the pandemic over time, we can repeatedly sample from key demographics and perform diagnostic testing. Representative sampling and antibody assays can also help estimate the number of previously infected individuals who may be immune to reinfection. This information can help to rule out the Oxford scenario in which the susceptible population is much, much smaller than we think. It can also help in estimating the infection fatality ratio, the proportion of COVID-19 patients who die from their infection. Ioannidis argues that the infection fatality ratio has been greatly overestimated in certain contexts due to biased testing. Antibody testing has already begun in the United States and other countries, including a (not yet peer-reviewed) study by Ioannidis and colleagues estimating much higher prevalence of past COVID-19 infections in Santa Clara County than the official count. Ironically, the study was immediately criticized by scientists partly for its Facebook recruitment strategy on the grounds it may have resulted in a biased sample.

The key to proper representative sampling is clinical epidemiology's favorite motto: randomize it! Random sampling can overcome the sampling bias that has plagued modeling projections alongside the coronavirus. The clinical epidemiology tradition, transfixed with unbiased evidence, provides a ready solution to an urgent problem facing public health epidemiology.

The final gift that clinical epidemiology offers is its skeptical disposition. Institutionalized skepticism is important in science and policymaking. Too much of it is paralyzing, especially in contexts of information poverty that call for pragmatism—like at the outset of a pandemic involving a novel pathogen when we don't have gold-standard evidence to guide us, but inaction carries the risk of dire consequences. But clinical epidemiology's skeptical orientation can provide a check on the pragmatic ethos of public health epidemiology, preventing action from outrunning evidence, or at least helping evidence to catch up.

At the same time, a myopic focus on evidence alone would do a disservice to epidemiology. Were we to conduct randomized trials of public health interventions, the evidence generated would be inherently local—specific to the context in which the trials are run—because the effects of public health interventions (really, all interventions) depend on what other causal factors are in play. We can't simply extrapolate from one context to another. Similarly, we should not blindly extrapolate infection statistics from one location to another; all these parameters—the reproductive number, the attack rate, the infection fatality ratio—are context-sensitive. None of these statistics is an intrinsic property of the virus or our interventions; they emerge from the interaction among intervention, pathogen, population, and place.

It is theory, along with a reliance on a diverse range of data, that make coronavirus evidence collected in one place relevant to another. Evidence for the effects of interventions on social interactions must be combined with outbreak models representing those interactions. Evidence for age-stratified infection fatality ratios must be combined with local data about the age structure of a population to be of any use in predicting fatalities in that population. In an outbreak, models without evidence are blind, while evidence without models is inert.

WHERE DOES THIS CLASH of sensibilities leave us? In my own work, I have modeled prediction in evidence-based medicine as a chain of inferences. Each individual inference is a link forged from assumptions in need of evidence; the chain is broken if any assumption breaks down. In their book *Evidence-Based Policy* (2012), philosopher of science Nancy Cartwright and economist Jeremy Hardie represent predictions about the effectiveness of a policy using a pyramid. The top level, the hypothesis that the policy will work in some local context, rests on several assumptions, which rest on further assumptions, and so on. Without evidence for the assumptions, the entire structure falls.

Either picture is a good metaphor for the relationship between evidence and models. Evidence is needed to support modeling assumptions to generate predictions that are more precise and accurate. Evidence is also needed to rule out alternative assumptions, and thus alternative predictions. Models represent a multiverse of hypothetical futures. Evidence helps us predict which future will materialize directly by filling in its contours, and indirectly by scratching out other hypothetical worlds.

The need for evidence and modeling will not dissolve when the dust settles in our future world. In evaluating the choices we made and the effectiveness of our policies, we will need to predict what would have happened otherwise. Such a judgment involves comparing worlds: the actual world that materialized and some hypothetical world that did not. How many COVID-19 deaths did our social distancing measures prevent? We can estimate the number of COVID-19 deaths in our actual socially distanced world by counting, but to predict the number of COVID-19 deaths in an unchosen world without social distancing, we will need to dust off our models and evidence.

Just as we should embrace both models and evidence, we should welcome both of epidemiology's competing philosophies. This may sound like a boring conclusion, but in the coronavirus pandemic there is no glory, and there are no winners. Cooperation in society should be matched by cooperation across disciplinary divides. The normal process of scientific scrutiny and peer review has given way to a fast track from research offices to media headlines and policy panels. Yet the need for criticism from diverse minds remains.

I mentioned that the discovery that smoking causes lung cancer was a discipline-defining achievement for public health epidemiology, while the British Medical Research Council's streptomycin trial was a formative episode in the history of clinical epidemiology. Epidemiologist Austin Bradford Hill played a role in both scientific achievements. He promoted the clinical trial in medicine and also provided nine criteria ("Hill's Viewpoints") still used in public health epidemiology for making causal inferences from a diversity of data.

Like Hill, epidemiology should be of two minds. It must combine theory with evidence and make use of diverse data while demanding data of increasingly higher quality. It must be liberal in its reasoning but conservative in its conclusions, pragmatic in its decision making while remaining skeptical of its own science. It must be split-brained, acting with one hand while collecting more information with the other. Only by borrowing from both ways of thinking will we have the right mind for a pandemic.

GOOD SCIENCE IS GOOD SCIENCE
Marc Lipsitch

MAY 12, 2020

BRAZILIAN-BRITISH BIOLOGIST PETER MEDAWAR won the Nobel Prize in 1960 for his study of acquired immune tolerance. Beyond his scientific work, he was also a gifted writer and expositor of scientific culture. One of the many treasures of his *Advice to a Young Scientist* (1979) is a passage in his chapter on "Aspects of Scientific Life and Manners" where he discusses "techniques used in the hope of enlarging one's reputation as a scientist or diminishing the reputation of others by nonscientific means."

One such "trick," Medawar writes, "is to affect the possession of a mind so finely critical that no evidence is ever quite good enough ('I am not very happy about . . .'; 'I must say I am not at all convinced by . . .')." After all, as he writes in a different passage, "no hypothesis in science and no scientific theory ever achieves . . . a degree of certainty beyond the reach of criticism or the possibility of modification."

I share Medawar's pragmatic vision of scientific reasoning. Scientists must resist the temptation to excessive skepticism: the kind that says no evidence is ever quite good enough. Instead they should keep their eyes open for any kind of information that can help them solve problems. Deciding, on principle, to reject some kinds of information outright, or to consider only particular kinds of studies, is counterproductive. Instead of succumbing to what Medawar calls "habitual disbelief," the scientist should pursue all possible inputs that can sharpen one's understanding, test one's preconceptions, suggest novel hypotheses, and identify previously unrecognized inconsistencies and limitations in one's view of a problem.

This conception of science leads me to disagree with some elements of philosopher of medicine Jonathan Fuller's essay about two sects within epidemiology, defined by what kinds of evidence they consider meaningful and how they think decisions should be made when evidence is uncertain. Fuller sees in the contrast two "competing philosophies" of scientific practice. One, he says, is characteristic of public health epidemiologists such as me, who are "methodologically liberal and pragmatic" and use models and diverse sources of data. The other, he explains, is characteristic of clinical epidemiologists such as Stanford's John Ioannidis, who draw on a tradition of skepticism about medical interventions in the literature of what has been known since the 1980s as "evidence-based medicine," privilege "gold standard" evidence from randomized controlled trials (as opposed to mere "data"), and counsel inaction until a certain ideal form of evidence—Evidence with a capital E—justifies intervening.

Fuller rightly points out that this distinction is only a rough approximation; indeed, there are many clinical epidemiologists who do not share the hardline skepticism associated with the most extreme wing of the evidence-based medicine community. But the distinction is also misleading in a subtle way. If the COVID-19 crisis has revealed two "competing" ways of thinking in distinct scientific traditions, it is not between two philosophies of *science* or two philosophies of *evidence* so much as between two philosophies of *action*.

In March, as health systems in Wuhan, Iran, and Northern Italy teetered under the weight of COVID-19 cases, Ioannidis cautioned that we really didn't know enough to say whether a response was appropriate, warning of a "once-in a-century evidence fiasco" and suggesting that the epidemic might dissipate "on its own." (I replied to that argument, explaining why we do know enough to act decisively against this pandemic.) To my knowledge, Ioannidis has never stated that early interventions should have been avoided, but by repeatedly criticizing the evidence on which they were based, he gives that impression.

On the question of how we interpret evidence, Fuller concludes that to understand the scientific disagreements being aired about COVID-19, we need to blend the insights of each camp. "Cooperation in society should be matched by cooperation across disciplinary divides," he writes. I don't understand what this kind of bothsidesism means when one side is characterized as accepting many types of evidence and the other as insisting on only certain kinds. On the question of how we should make decisions under uncertainty, of course more data are better. But decisions are urgent and must be made with the evidence we have.

This is not to deny that there are different and valuable perspectives on epidemiology. Like any other field, there are many specialties and subspecialties. They have different methods for how they study the world, how they analyze data, and how they filter new information. No one person can keep up with the flood of scientific information in even one field, and specialization is necessary for progress: different scientists need to use different approaches given their skills, interests, and resources. But specialization should not lead to sects—in this case, a group of scientists who accept only certain kinds of evidence and too rigidly adhere to a philosophy of noninterventionism.

INFECTIOUS DISEASE EPIDEMIOLOGISTS must embrace diverse forms of evidence by the very nature of their subject. We study a wide range of questions: how and under what conditions infectious diseases are transmitted, how pathogens change genetically as they spread among populations and across regions, how those changes affect our health, and how our immune systems protect us and, sometimes, make us vulnerable to severe illness when immune responses get out of control. We also seek to understand what kinds of control measures are most effective in limiting transmission. To understand these issues for even *one* type of disease—say, coronavirus diseases—requires drawing on a wide range of methodologies and disciplines.

We consider evidence from classical *epidemiological* studies of transmission in households and other settings. We consider *immunological* studies that show us how markers of immunity develop, whether they protect us against future disease, and how particular markers (say a certain type of antibody directed at a certain part of the virus) change infection and mortality rates. We consider *molecular genetics* experiments, including those conducted in animal models, that tell us how changes in a virus's genome affect the course of disease. We consider evolutionary patterns in the virus's genetic code, seasonal patterns in its transmission and that of other related viruses, and observational studies of the risk factors and circumstances favoring transmission. And, of course, we also consider randomized trials of treatments and prevention measures, when they exist, as we seek to understand which interventions work and which ones may do more harm than good.

The upshot is that, done well, epidemiology synthesizes many branches of science using many methods, approaches, and forms of evidence. No one can be expert in all of these specialties, and few can even be conversant in all of them. But a scientist should be open to learning about all of these kinds of evidence and more.

Thinking about evidence from diverse specialties is critical not only for weighing evidence and deciding how to act but also for developing hypotheses that, when tested, can shed light across specialties. Appropriate humility dictates that molecular virologists should not assume they are experts in social epidemiology, and vice versa. To say "I'm a virologist, so I'm not going to account for any findings from social epidemiology in my work" gives up the chance to understand the world better.

Here's an example. In the case of a new virus such as SARS-CoV-2, the fact that socioeconomically disadvantaged people get sick more often than the wealthy gives clues—which we don't yet know how to interpret—about the way the virus interacts with hosts. It would be informative to a virologist to distinguish the following two hypotheses (among others): (a) exposure to high doses of virus tends to cause severe disease, and disadvantaged people are often exposed to higher doses due to confined living and working conditions, or (b) comorbidities such as heart disease and obesity are higher among disadvantaged people, and lead to more severe outcomes. Of course, either, both, or neither of these hypotheses may turn out to be important explanations, but the canny virologist should wonder and think about how to distinguish them experimentally and test results against data from human populations. Reciprocally, a canny social epidemiologist should look to virological studies for clues about why COVID-19, like so many other illnesses, disproportionately harms the least advantaged in our society.

In practice, virologists, immunologists, and epidemiologists are different specialists who often work far apart and almost never attend each other's seminars. I do not think we should spend all our time learning each other's disciplines. But I do think that a scientist who genuinely wants to solve an important problem should be open to evidence from many sources, should welcome the opportunity to expand their list of hypotheses, and should seek to increase their chances both of making a novel contribution to their field and of being right. Central to this effort is considering information from diverse kinds of studies performed by people with diverse job titles in diverse departments of the university—as well as their diverse forms of data and argumentation.

When we move from the realm of understanding to the realm of intervention, the need for openness to different sources of evidence grows further. In some cases—whether to use a drug to treat infection, say, or whether to use a mask to prevent transmission—we can draw on evidence from experiments, sometimes even randomized, controlled, double-blind experiments. But in deciding whether to impose social distancing during an outbreak of a novel pathogen—and in thinking about how the course of the epidemic might play out—it would be crazy not to consider whatever data we can, including from mathematical models and from other epidemics throughout history. With infectious diseases, especially new and fast-spreading pandemics, action can't wait for the degree of evidentiary purity we get from fully randomized and controlled experiments, or from the ideal observational study. At the same time, we must continue to improve our understanding while we act and change our actions as our knowledge changes—leaving both our beliefs and our actions open, as Medawar says, to the reach of criticism and the possibility of modification.

WHERE DOES THE SKEPTICISM so characteristic of the evidence-based tradition come from? One reason may be the habits and heuristics we absorb from textbooks, colleagues, and mentors.

In supervising students and postdocs, inculcating these habits is one of the most challenging, gratifying, and time-consuming parts of scientific training—far more than teaching technical skills. Some of these rules of thumb are well suited to science in general and serve us well throughout our careers, no matter the field. Among these are workaday but important heuristics such as: consider alternative hypotheses; look at raw data whenever possible before looking at processed data; and repeat experiments, especially those whose results surprise you. Indeed, these heuristics can be summarized as a form of intense skepticism directed at one's *own* work and that of one's team: find all the flaws you can before someone else does; fix those you can and highlight as limitations those which are unfixable. Recently an advanced PhD student said to me: "I read your new idea that you shared on Slack this morning and I've been doing my best all afternoon to break it." It made my day, and made me think I probably had very little left to teach her.

Other heuristics, however, are more specific to a narrow field and may be ill suited to other contexts. Insisting on gold-standard, randomized trial evidence *before* prescribing drugs to prevent heart attacks or performing a certain surgical operation may be a good rule of thumb in medicine (though not all physicians or even philosophers agree). But randomized controlled trials are not available for huge swaths of scientific inquiry, and the narrow populations often studied in such trials can limit their applicability to real-world decision-making. Nor are they always available when we need them: they require a lot of time and administrative resources to execute (and money, for that matter). Stumping for Evidence is thus useful in many parts of clinical medicine but impractical in many other aspects of science-informed decision-making. Applying this doctrine indiscriminately across all areas of science turns the tools of a specialist into the weapons of a sectarian.

This point was appreciated by some of the pioneers of evidence-based medicine: David Sackett, William Rosenberg, J. A. Muir

Gray, R. Brian Haynes, and W. Scott Richardson. "Evidence-based medicine is not restricted to randomized trials and meta-analyses," they wrote in 1996. "It involves tracking down the best external evidence with which to answer our clinical questions." And last week Oxford professor of primary care Trisha Greenhalgh, another major contributor to this field and author of a popular textbook on evidence-based medicine, suggested that in the realm of social interventions to control the spread of COVID-19, the evidence-based clinical paradigm—"waiting for the definitive [randomized controlled trial] before taking action"—"should not be seen as inviolable, or as always defining good science."

Indeed, on the question of how we ought to act during an outbreak, two leading epidemiologists in the clinical tradition, Hans-Olov Adami and the late Dimitrios Trichopoulos, argued that the noninterventionist rule of thumb is suitable for chronic, noncommunicable diseases but foolish for fast-moving infectious diseases. In an editorial accompanying an article that showed that the impact of cell phones in causing brain cancer was not large but might be larger than zero, they counseled "cautious inaction" in regulating cell phones. But they noted this is not how you would reason in the case of a transmissible disease:

> There is another lesson to be learned about the alarms that have been sounded about public health during the past few years. When the real or presumed risk involves communicable agents, such as the prions that cause bovine spongiform encephalopathy (mad cow disease), no precaution, however extreme, can be considered excessive. By contrast, for noncommunicable agents, such as radio-frequency energy, the lack

of a theoretical foundation and the absence of empirical evidence of a substantial increase in risk legitimize cautious inaction, unless and until a small excess risk is firmly documented.

I would tone down the statement that "no precaution, however extreme, can be considered excessive," which is either rhetorical or sectarian. But in my ideal public health world, we'd have a lot more good sense like that proposed by Adami and Trichopoulos, acting not only on the strength of the evidence we have but on the relative harms of being wrong in each direction. And whether waiting or acting, we'd work hard to get the evidence to meet the challenges of skeptics and improve our decision-making, all with an eye to the possibility of criticism and modification Medawar describes.

What does all this mean for the COVID-19 crisis? Scientists of all stripes should work together to improve public health, and none should mistake a professional tendency or a specialist's rule of thumb for an unshakable epistemological principle. All should support rigorous evidence gathering, especially for the costliest and most disruptive interventions. And insofar as scientists identify with a philosophical school that predisposes them to write off certain forms of evidence entirely, they should, in short, get over it. Instead we should use every possible source of insight at our disposal to gain knowledge and inform decisions, which are always made under uncertainty—rarely more so than at present.

THE TOTALITY OF THE EVIDENCE
John P. A. Ioannidis

MAY 26, 2020

A PERSON SUDDENLY COLLAPSES—what do you do? Given the choice between acting or not acting, surely every reasonable person will say we need to act without hesitation.

But how? We first quickly collect the available data: we check whether the collapsed person has a pulse, whether he's breathing, whether he responds to verbal cues. If not, we suspect cardiac arrest and immediately start CPR—but still we try to collect both new and better data as we go along. If a blood pressure monitor becomes available and we find the patient's pressure is fine and his pulse is regular—though we didn't even feel one at first—everything changes; the situation is not as dire as we had thought. Perhaps he begins talking, though his breathing is still labored: our chest compressions have broken his ribs. If we don't stop CPR, the bone may pierce his lungs, causing a tension pneumothorax—a life-threatening condition that must be treated right away. Despite our best intentions, we can kill the patient if we do not change our course of action.

The first question in emergencies, this example teaches, is not *whether* to act. It is rather *how* to act to ensure our actions do more good than harm. Populations are not individual patients, of course, but the lesson is important for thinking about the debate over the right response to the COVID-19 crisis. Philosopher of medicine Jonathan Fuller sheds light on this debate by describing two opposing traditions in epidemiology: one, public health epidemiology, that relies on modeling and a diversity of data, and another, clinical epidemiology, that prizes high-quality evidence from randomized studies. In an equally thoughtful response, epidemiologist Marc Lipsitch elaborates on what that opposition gets wrong.

Both Fuller and Lipsitch have eloquently expressed the simultaneously competing and coexisting worlds of models and evidence. I hope that we would all agree that we need both. Science is difficult; we cannot afford to look away from useful data, disciplines, approaches, and methods. I love science because most of the time I feel profoundly ignorant, in need of continuous education; I am grateful to all my colleagues—no matter their discipline—who help reduce my ignorance. At the same time, we should study the strengths, weaknesses, and complementarity of various approaches. The main challenge in epidemiology, in particular, is how to translate what we know—and what we know about what we know—into the best course of action.

As Lipsitch suggests, infectious disease epidemiology and clinical epidemiology are not necessarily two opposing stereotypes; almost always they are intermingled. And as Fuller acknowledges in passing, they can coexist in the same research agenda, in the same institution, even in the same person. Most scientists cannot be slotted in one bin or the other; they struggle to make their brains work in different paradigms. Both essays classify me under the evidence-based medicine (EBM) umbrella, but while it is true that I have written papers with "evidence-based medicine" in the title, I have no official degree in EBM. When I trained in the field with the late Tom Chalmers and Joseph Lau, there were no degrees of that sort. The term "evidence-based medicine" itself wasn't coined until 1992 by clinical epidemiologists at McMaster University in Canada. Even now, almost thirty years later, in most places most scientists and physicians still have no clue what EBM really is. My official fellowship training, in fact, was in infectious diseases.

Regardless of the difficulty of classifying scientists in bins, however, science does work eventually, as researchers share knowledge and correct misconceptions. And even if we take the stereotypes of the two traditions for granted, their features ought to be reversed in one respect. In a certain sense, it is clinical epidemiology that tends to be more pragmatic, and thus more action-oriented, than its foil. Traditional epidemiology—including research programs on mechanisms of disease—can be far removed from questions of action, for good reason: basic science has great value in itself for learning about nature and modeling its mysteries. By contrast, EBM, in particular, argues for less theory and more real-world results, less speculation and more focus on the outcomes that matter most. To put it crudely but sharply, the EBM sensibility is that theories don't count for much when they don't save lives. That process of saving lives focuses on decisions of action. Practitioners of EBM know full well that failing to act has consequences; a central lesson that it teaches is that you'd better choose wisely what you do—and what you don't.

What does all this mean in the case of COVID-19? On March 3, the World Health Organization (WHO) director-general introduced a media briefing with these distressing words: "Globally, about 3.4 percent of reported COVID-19 cases have died. By comparison, seasonal flu generally kills far fewer than 1 percent of those infected." Others spoke of a very high reproduction number, of almost no asymptomatic infections, and of the high likelihood that the virus would infect most of the global population. Many, including the team led by Neil Ferguson at Imperial College London, drew comparisons to the 1918 pandemic, which cost at least 50 million lives globally. These claims had a dramatic and arguably dangerous impact on public perception. Moreover, if these claims had been true, any EBM practitioner would call for swift and thoroughgoing lockdown measures. EBM is dead clear in such situations: if the risk is 50 million deaths, shutting the world for a month or two is nothing.

But it was my infectious disease side that had questions. A virus that spreads like wildfire, killing one out of thirty and infecting almost everyone in the absence of a vaccine, should have killed far more people in China and should have spread widely worldwide, perhaps with millions of fatalities, by mid-March. Hence, as I wrote in an op-ed in Stat News, I began to plead that we seek to obtain better data as quickly as possible to best inform our actions. I think lockdown was justified as an initial response, given what little we knew about this new virus, but I also think we needed better data to decide on next steps. Given what we know now, it is reasonable to consider alternatives to population-wide lockdown, even as we continue preventive hygiene measures, exercise local infection controls, focus on protecting those most at risk, and support health care systems to care for patients who are sick.

Two and a half months after COVID-19 was officially declared a pandemic, we lament a great and acute loss of life, especially in places such as Lombardy and New York. Since the outbreak was detected in Wuhan in December 2019, the global death toll is estimated to be 346,000 as of this writing. But because our interventions can harm as well as help, it is not unreasonable to put this number in context.

We now know that the death toll is not comparable to that of the 1918 pandemic. We also now know that the virus has spread widely, but for the vast majority of people it is far less lethal than we thought: it kills far fewer than 3.4 percent of those who develop symptoms. Late last week the CDC adopted an estimated death rate of 0.4 percent for those who develop symptoms and acknowledged that there are many other infected people who develop no symptoms at all. These estimates will continue to improve as time goes on, but it is clear that the numbers are much lower than first feared. The exact infection fatality rate varies across populations and settings, but it appears that in most situations outside nursing homes and hospitals, it tends to be very low.

We have learned that COVID-19 is yet another disease that unfortunately and disproportionately affects the elderly, the disadvantaged, and those with multiple underlying medical conditions. Besides massacring nursing homes, and having the potential to infect many vulnerable patients and providers in hospitals, it painfully emerges as yet another disease of inequality. The poor, the homeless, people in prisons, low-wage workers in meat-processing plants, and other essential jobs are among the hardest hit, while privileged people like me are videoconferencing in safety. That is a tragic disparity.

At the same time, we should not look away from the real harms of the most drastic of our interventions, which also disproportionately affect the disadvantaged. We know that prolonged lockdown of the entire population has delayed cancer treatments and has made people with serious diseases such as heart attacks avoid going to the hospital. It is leading hospital systems to furlough and lay off personnel, it is devastating mental health, it is increasing domestic violence and child abuse, and it has added at least 36.5 million new people to the ranks of the unemployed in the United States alone. Many of these people will lose health insurance, putting them at further risk of declining health and economic distress. Prolonged unemployment is estimated to lead to an extra 75,000 deaths of despair in the United States alone over the coming decade. At a global level, disruption has increased the number of people at risk of starvation to more than a billion, suspension of mass vaccination campaigns is posing a threat of resurgence of infectious diseases that kill children, modeling suggests an excess of 1.4 million deaths from tuberculosis by 2025, and a doubling of the death toll from malaria in 2020 is expected compared with 2018. I hope these modeling predictions turn out to be as wrong as several COVID-19 modeling predictions have, but they may not. All of these impacts matter, too. Policymakers must consider the harms of restrictive policies, not just their benefits.

Good science can come from public health epidemiology, from the study of infectious diseases, from evidence-based medicine, from clinical epidemiology, or from any discipline. I agree with Lipsitch that we need to respect the *totality* of the evidence—including, I would stress, evidence about the harms of prolonged lockdown—rather than rely too narrowly on the claims of any one disciplinary specialty. At the beginning, in the absence of high-quality data, we can do what seems most reasonable, following the precautionary principle and using common sense. But beyond this point, failing to correct our ignorance and adapt our actions as quickly as possible is not good science. Nor is politicizing scientific disagreement or looking away from the undeniable harms of our well-intentioned actions.

FROM PANDEMIC FACTS TO PANDEMIC POLICIES
Jonathan Fuller

JUNE 2, 2020

WITH OVER 100,000 DEATHS in the United States and over 370,000 deaths worldwide after five months, the COVID-19 pandemic is the health crisis of a generation. Yet even while the crisis unfolds, it is important to step back and reflect on the science helping decision-makers navigate the uncertain and the unknown.

It is with that goal in mind that I offered a philosophical perspective on two epidemiological traditions now at the center of public discussion, each roughly associated with a distinct philosophy of scientific knowledge. Two epidemiologists I named in the piece, Marc Lipsitch and John Ioannidis, have now responded. Elsewhere, Lipsitch and Ioannidis have disagreed on the use of lockdowns and strict social distancing in the pandemic. Going against the grain, Ioannidis has questioned their justification; Lipsitch, siding with the majority of epidemiologists, has argued they are justified. Regarding our exchange, I draw three conclusions.

First, at a high resolution what constitutes good science might differ according to the scientific field, and we should not apply evidence-based medicine's standards for evidence to public health science. Second, it is not only the scientific facts (including the grim death toll) that are at issue, but also the less often discussed relationship between science and decision-making, where values inevitably play a role. And third, that weighing harms and benefits of proposed policies is not straightforward, and it demands the same rigor used in modeling and generating evidence.

The Varieties of Scientific Experience

BOTH LIPSITCH AND IOANNIDIS reinforced my caveat that it can be difficult to fit any given scientist into one or either of the two intellectual boxes I described and that a single scientist can operate in these different modes at different times. The distinct philosophies I identified are norms of thinking imprinted on different schools or specialties in epidemiology, not inviolable codes. The evidence-based medicine (EBM) philosophy is neatly crystallized by the hierarchy of evidence, which places systematic reviews of randomized intervention studies at the top of a pyramid of evidence types. The public health epidemiology philosophy is embodied in Hill's Viewpoints, nine guidelines for inferring causation from association that collectively call upon a plurality of kinds of research.

I agree with Lipsitch that rigid sectarianism is counterproductive to science; my discussion of the two philosophies was a description rather than an endorsement. Elements of both philosophies can be virtues. They are more likely to be virtuous when they are balanced with each other: models with high-quality evidence, data diversity with data quality, pragmatism with skepticism. This balance does not require different disciplines privileging different elements; science is at its best when it embraces all of them. However, as Lipsitch describes there is also great diversity among sciences. While there might be very general features of good science—it remains unsettled in philosophy as to exactly what these features might be—at a higher level of resolution that captures day-to-day scientific practice, what constitutes good science in one discipline might not be good science in another, owing to differences in the domain of study or the uses to which scientific results are put.

Lipsitch suggests that the cooperation I advocate among the two schools is incomprehensible if epidemiologists cling to contradictory principles, the former accepting a diversity of evidence while the latter insists on only randomized studies. Instead he endorses evidential diversity in the response to the coronavirus pandemic and wards off the attempt to apply rigid standards of evidence from the "most extreme wing of the evidence-based medicine community." While I welcome EBM's emphasis on evidence, data quality, and skepticism (when appropriately applied), I wholeheartedly agree that in all of epidemiology and science—including clinical epidemiology—we must be pluralists about evidence and prediction, partly because different kinds of evidence support different assumptions in our scientific reasoning. In another recent essay, for example, EBM researcher Trisha Greenhalgh argues that some EBM experts have made crucial mistakes in the pandemic by applying EBM's orthodox standards of evidence for medical therapies to public health interventions, particularly mask-wearing.

The Interface of Science and Policy

BEYOND THE PHILOSOPHICAL DIMENSIONS of epidemic models and epidemiological evidence, these essays also call our attention to the complex relationship between science and action. Lipsitch and Ioannidis appear to disagree not only about certain strictly scientific matters, but also about practical decision-making under uncertainty —what actions are supported by the science. This distinction often gets overlooked in public discussions that focus solely on scientific studies—including studies authored or coauthored by Ioannidis, which have been widely and roundly criticized by other scientists. As a result, so much of Ioannidis's tussle with mainstream opinion in epidemiology and public health has been portrayed as a disagreement over scientific facts. It is that, but it is also more than that.

Consider the specific controversy overestimates of SARS-CoV-2's infection fatality ratio (IFR). Ioannidis claims in his own research that, worldwide, the IFR may be near the value for seasonal influenza. But even if Ioannidis turns out to be correct (which many experts have doubted), no policy prescription immediately follows, certainly not the idea that our response to the two viruses should be similar (which Ioannidis has not, to my knowledge, argued). For one thing, the IFR does not on its own represent the dangerousness of the virus. It is only one variable determining the number of deaths, which is the product of the IFR and the number of infections (the latter has the potential to be vastly greater for coronavirus compared to seasonal flu because SARS-CoV-2 has never infected humans before). The number of lives at stake should more directly inform decision-making rather than the IFR itself, but even here the gap between number and action is large.

It is worth remembering, therefore, that models and evidence are not the only inputs into the decision-making process. Values are also needed to animate the facts and move decision-makers to action. Public health decisions are infused with values, even when those values are unacknowledged and only implicit. These values trickle down to influence the science informing public health. As a result, it is wrong to say that decision-makers (as well as epidemiologists advocating for or against public health measures) are just "following the science." They are taking political action that is as much informed by social and political values as it is by science. There is thus an urgent need for transparency not only regarding the facts—what models and evidence are informing the response and what predictions they yield—but also regarding the values linking them to action. In the absence of such clarity, disagreements over values or policy may masquerade as disagreements over science or facts.

One way values enter into scientific practice is via the outcomes researchers choose to measure in generating evidence and constructing models. One study might measure aggregate outcomes such as the total number of deaths in a population, while an analysis more attuned to health inequities—such as those that have fallen along lines of race and socioeconomic status in the current pandemic—might be more concerned with the distribution of outcomes across population subgroups. These are but a few of the value-laden decisions that precede the decision of what interventions to use. Selecting the "best" policy is partly a matter of science, then, but it is also inevitably a matter of values, too.

The Challenges of Cost-Benefit Analysis

A FINAL INSIGHT to be gained from this exchange concerns the complexities of cost-benefit analysis. Ioannidis's main argument against population-wide "lockdowns"—presumably referring to shelter-in-place and stay-at-home orders—in his reply to my essay seems to take this form. He believes the benefits of lockdown have been exaggerated due partly to overestimating the IFR and to comparisons to the 1918 flu pandemic. Meanwhile, he suggests that the potential harms of lockdown have been overlooked, including effects such as delayed and averted treatment for other diseases, increased violence in the home and compromised mental health, more suicides and deaths from substance abuse, interrupted vaccination campaigns, increased global food insecurity, and increased deaths from tuberculosis and malaria in lower income countries. On balance, he concludes, lockdown could very well be inferior to other policy alternatives, which we should accordingly consider. Ioannidis does not go as far as to say that lockdown *is* inferior, but I read him as intimating that this conclusion is a strong possibility.

Although the value of cost-benefit analysis is not uncontroversial, especially when the relevant harms and benefits are qualitatively different, I accept that it is a reasonable approach, while noting that there are many ways of carrying it out. Its use need not be restricted to polarized, far-apart alternatives; it could be applied to more fine-grained decisions such as which businesses to permit to reopen and on what dates. I will close by pointing out a few gaps in Ioannidis's harm-benefit argument, which will serve to illustrate some of the difficulties of decision-making in the pandemic.

First, although Ioannidis does not consider specific alternatives in his response, a harm-benefit analysis is only useful in the context of decision-making if it is contrastive: that is, if it compares one policy to others. Even *if* it were the case that the harms of lockdown are more severe than the harms of some alternatives, its benefits compared to those alternatives might still outweigh its harms.

Second, assessing the harms of our interventions relies on causal inference. But we can only causally attribute harms and benefits to lockdown through comparative empirical analysis, for instance by modeling alternative scenarios or generating comparative evidence of an intervention's effectiveness. Such an analysis might well reveal that an outcome is not (or not primarily) due to lockdown; it might have arisen either way, for instance due to people voluntarily social distancing in fear of the virus. Ioannidis argues that the imperative to respect all the evidence should include evidence of the harms of our interventions. I would add that this evidence must consider the counterfactual: what would have happened under some alternative scenario.

Third, an intervention's harms must be considered in the context of further actions we can take to mitigate them. The harms or side effects of noxious chemotherapies, including nausea, can sometimes be offset—if only partially—through other treatments, and the existence of such side effect treatments should be considered in a harm-benefit analysis comparing different chemotherapies. Likewise, a harm-benefit analysis of public health measures must consider what supplementary interventions exist to counteract the social ills induced: economic, health-related, or otherwise.

Finally, a harm-benefit analysis demands more than a back-of-the-envelope treatment; it deserves as much rigor as goes into epidemic modeling or estimating model parameters. Neither the coronavirus pandemic nor our interventions and their effects are purely biological; they are psychological and social as well. Thus, harm-benefit analysis, and decision-making more generally in the pandemic, must involve a diverse range of experts—a much wider array than the two kinds of epidemiologist I initially described. On this need for diverse expertise, I think Lipsitch, Ioannidis, and I all agree.

PANDEMIC POLICY

Case
Studies

RECESSIONS OFTEN IMPROVE POPULATION HEALTH, BUT COVID-19 MAY BE DIFFERENT

Sarah Burgard & Lucie Kalousova

APRIL 15, 2020

AS THE ECONOMIC DEVASTATION of the COVID-19 pandemic is becoming painfully evident—already some 17 million workers have filed for unemployment benefits in the United States—questions are arising about how the emerging recession will further impact population health. Though many as-yet-unanswerable questions remain, we are likely to see a mix of negative and positive health consequences.

Thanks to a revival of research and debate in the wake of the Great Recession, we know that recessions lead to short-term improvement in life expectancy at the population level, but also to declining well-being for those individuals who experience labor market, housing, and asset shocks. However, never in living memory have we faced this one-two punch of a massive health crisis triggering an economic one. Predictions based on past experience must tread cautiously if we are to make the best use of existing scholarship and policy strategies to mitigate the population health consequences of the coming recession.

We should start with what we know from past economic downturns. Though it may seem counterintuitive, evidence from around the world has shown that the mortality rate *falls* relatively quickly in recessions, and consequently that life expectancy *rises*. Most evidence has come from milder downturns, but the same pattern was also found for the Great Depression in the United States. What explains this "silver lining" of past recessions for population health? With the deceleration in business and industrial activity, commuting and air pollution fall, leading to a drop in traffic-related fatalities and cardiovascular deaths. There is already evidence that the pollution burden in cities such as Los Angeles has been radically reduced in the wake of stay-at-home orders and the shutdown of many businesses and social activities.

Beyond the environmental changes that provide broad reductions in health risk, other ways we respond to recessions could lead to improvements or reductions in population health. Some scholars have argued that the time regained when people face work slowdowns or unemployment allows for more leisure, physical activity, home cooking, and other behaviors that could enhance well-being. A shock to disposable income could also reduce consumption of tobacco or alcohol. Counterbalancing these positive effects are the stress and uncertainty of financial strain and psychological distress, which may lead to less than optimal use of new free time (such as sedentary television viewing), may reduce work-related physical and social activities, and could also increase negative coping with tobacco or alcohol, particularly for those who already use them regularly.

The most consistent negative population health consequence of recessions is a rise in suicide mortality. Such a pattern is devastating but not surprising, given the stress and material hardships associated with the kinds of events that increase during economic downturns—including job losses, long-term unemployment, and loss of financial and housing assets. Stress has also been shown to be associated with increased inflammation, reduced immunity, and lower levels of mental well-being, all factors that threaten health.

WHILE THERE IS CONSIDERABLE RESEARCH to draw on as we speculate about the health impacts of the COVID-19 recession, the situation we face now makes it risky to rely only on past experiences. Consider three of the most obvious differences that distinguish the COVID-19 era.

First, this recession is being triggered by a global viral pandemic that threatens many of the usual "silver linings" of economic downturn. Stay-at-home orders and closures of nonessential businesses keep us from many of the activities we might have more healthfully traded for paid work or commuting, such as going to the gym, spending time outdoors, or socializing with friends. Lockdown also means that in-person social and instrumental support we typically provide or receive from others may be curtailed, increasing isolation and making health maintenance—physical as well as mental—more challenging. It may also be difficult to devote more time to healthful behaviors such as adequate sleep (in homes overcrowded by shelter-mates) or cooking healthy meals (if groceries are difficult to get). And parents across the country who are still employed are struggling to manage both their paid jobs and the very challenging work of caring for and educating their children.

Second, the health care sector has been decimated by COVID-19, with facilities overwhelmed, essential supplies limited, and health care providers strained beyond normal limits. Tragically, many health care providers have been sickened and even killed by the virus, and those still on the front lines are desperate for more support and safe conditions. These circumstances will leave our health care system frail even after the first wave of the virus has abated, precisely when a wave of delayed procedures and treatments are being sought. Our ability to increase health care system capacity will be important in the fight against future waves of viral outbreak, but budgets may not accommodate expansions. The capacity of preventive public health systems will also be constrained in the coming months, and a great deal of scientific activity will be diverted to attempts to control the virus—leaving fewer resources for other important public health functions. Beyond the budgetary strain, another tragic consequence of COVID-19 is the cessation of mass vaccination against preventable diseases such as polio and measles, given the risk of viral transmission in such face-to-face efforts. Exhausted and financially strapped health care and public health systems will make it even harder to maintain the population's health as the economy falters and recovery attempts are made.

Third, sudden changes in what makes a job dangerous could stymie traditional paths to economic recovery, and they are both revealing and exacerbating deep social inequalities. More advantaged Americans are likelier to have the option to work from home, the resources to adapt to new and rapidly changing expectations, and the assets to weather what is likely to be a long storm. By contrast, COVID-19 has dealt devastating blows to a low-wage workforce already facing health disadvantages, and communities of color are bearing a disproportionate number of fatalities. If low-wage workers are sickened because they cannot afford not to work in a pandemic, or because they do not have the ability to safely self-quarantine, who will staff the massive share of low-wage service jobs when the economic engines start up again? One of the "silver linings" of past recessions was a decline in workplace accidents, presumably because the most experienced or qualified workers kept their jobs and a slower pace of production allowed for more attention to worker safety. A cruelty of this highly transmissible disease is that simply being at the workplace can pose health risks, and it does so at a time when attention to traditional workplace hazards is not likely on the radar.

Given these differences, where are we likely headed in these unprecedented times? Several factors suggest that the normally health-enhancing aspects of recessions may be weaker and overall population health impact more negative. Even before this economic downturn, U.S. data suggested a weakening of the traditional recession-induced life expectancy bump. One proposed explanation for that weakening has been the increasing role of cancer in driving overall mortality rates. In the past, cancer deaths were only weakly related to the business cycle, but that relationship may be strengthening as the affordability of new and effective cancer treatments declines in tough economic times. It is too early to tell how drastically the pandemic will shape the cause of death profile in the coming months and years, and how much this will influence the historically consistent association between personal economic resources and health. Further examination of emerging overall and cause-specific mortality patterns, and of the mechanisms that underlie them, will be critical to understand whether COVID-19 will change the nature of the link between recessions and life expectancy in the United States.

Another factor working against a population health "silver lining" is that older Americans are at greater risk of mortality. Even if they do not contract the virus, those who face other health problems typical of later life are at greater than normal risk because the surge of attention and resources toward COVID-19 may delay necessary care and lessen survival associated with other causes. Health among survivors may also be compromised by the challenges of sheltering in place, from an increased risk of domestic violence to the harmful effects of spending long periods of time exposed to environmental hazards for those living in poorly maintained and crowded housing. Some of these hazards are unequally felt by poor Americans, potentially widening existing disparities by income, race, ethnicity, gender, and other social characteristics.

The health impacts of the COVID-19 downturn will also depend on the precise nature of the economic recovery—how quickly and effectively the record-shattering unemployment claims of the past few weeks are reversed. Policies to maintain workers on payrolls even during a slowdown or to support businesses that will be able to rehire them can lessen the damaging social, economic, and health consequences of long-term unemployment, but the need for social distancing and the resulting devastation of many industries make this much more challenging. Individually directed stimulus funds will be a welcome relief to cash-strapped Americans, but it is less likely they will stimulate the economy as they would in a typical recession.

This is to say nothing of the health effects outside of the United States. We know very little about how economic recessions are linked to population health in developing countries; most research has been conducted in wealthy ones. However, there is cause for concern. While there is already evidence that air pollution is falling sharply in cities across the globe, residents of many urban metropolises face much greater challenges in adequately physically distancing due to residential crowding and poorer quality housing stock, potentially stretching out the duration of the epidemic and the associated recession.

Additionally, the severe short-run lack of personal protective equipment and intensive care unit beds to deal with surges of patients will add to the toll of mortality. In the longer run, many poorer nations have even fewer financial resources to backstop overloaded health care systems and to provide social safety nets during economic downturns. Many countries will also suffer from declining revenues from tourism, from dwindling remittances from household members working abroad, and from challenges to systems of migratory labor that have supported economic well-being in many communities.

HOW CAN WE BEST PREPARE for the downturn's health effects? We should certainly pursue extensions to social welfare programs including food stamps and unemployment insurance: these are powerful tools that reduced material hardship in the Great Recession and that can help even under shutdown conditions. Protecting jobs and households from health-harming food insecurity and financial strain is a start. Rent and mortgage freezes, extended moratoria on evictions, and forgiveness or extended grace periods on all forms of student loans are other ways to ease the financial strain facing so many Americans. However, we must also think beyond short-term, stopgap measures. The COVID-19 pandemic reveals deep fault lines in our economic norms, social safety net, and public health infrastructure, laying bare persistent health disparities across social groups.

This unprecedented set of circumstances provides an opportunity to innovate in ways that will support population health as we face future waves of COVID-19 and other social, environmental, and health crises. One line of reform should involve better social policies. Distribution of social welfare assistance through cash transfers, food stamps, unemployment assistance, and housing assistance could be bolstered and simplified in ways that help poorer families handle more typical shocks to employment or health. We must also consider the human and economic costs of lacking adequate health insurance, as this pandemic has revealed the risks to the entire population of uninsured individuals avoiding testing for COVID-19 for fear of an unaffordable bill or failing to access appropriate care when experiencing symptoms. We could also take advantage of more widespread recognition of the value of paid sick leave, a benefit that so many Americans lack, but one that could greatly enhance individuals' ability to stay home and heal, or care for loved ones who are ill.

Finally, we must also work to tackle systemic issues underlying inequitable health outcomes. Reports have shown COVID-19 to have a disproportionately large mortality rate among Black Americans, for whom generations of structural racism have left their communities more vulnerable to the chronic health conditions that make COVID-19 particularly deadly. Addressing these and other longstanding health disparities, as well as our social welfare and public health systems, could make Americans more resilient to the population health challenges we already face and the new ones that will arise.

HYDROXYCHLOROQUINE AND THE POLITICAL POLARIZATION OF SCIENCE

Cailin O'Connor & James Owen Weatherall

MAY 4, 2020

ON JANUARY 29 the *Hubei Daily*, a state-owned Chinese newspaper based in Wuhan, reported on a promising development. Teams of researchers associated with the Chinese Academy of Military Medical Sciences and the Wuhan Institute of Virology had tested dozens of existing pharmaceuticals for possible efficacy against the novel coronavirus. They had identified three antiviral drugs that seemed to inhibit the virus from reproducing or infecting other cells in a test tube.

Within a week the highly regarded journal, *Cell Research*, published a peer-reviewed letter by researchers at the Wuhan Institute of Virology that reported on two of these in more detail: chloroquine, developed in the 1930s to treat malaria, and remdesivir, a newer drug developed for Ebola. Within days Chinese researchers announced new clinical studies to test these drugs in patients, along with another antimalarial drug, hydroxychloroquine, which is derived from chloroquine and is generally considered safer. The science has continued apace, and results of most of the clinical studies are still pending.

In the meantime, something strange happened. It started with a series of tweets. On March 11 an Australian entrepreneur living in China tweeted at a Bitcoin investor that chloroquine would "keep most people out of hospital." That investor then coauthored and shared a document making the case for chloroquine. On March 16 Elon Musk began tweeting about chloroquine and hydroxychloroquine and shared that document. Two days later Tucker Carlson did a segment on Fox News discussing these drugs with one of the document's coauthors. That same day, March 19, President Donald Trump gave a press conference in which he announced that chloroquine and hydroxychloroquine had shown "very, very encouraging" early results. Since then, Trump has repeatedly touted hydroxychloroquine as a COVID-19 miracle drug.

Over the following weeks, the question of whether hydroxychloroquine is a safe and effective treatment for COVID-19 became a locus for political tribalism and polarization. Trump supporters on social media share evidence, often anecdotal or clinical, that hydroxychloroquine is effective; Trump's critics share evidence that it is not and argue there are significant costs to promoting an unproven drug. Even traditional media has weighed in. The right-leaning *Wall Street Journal* published an opinion piece by doctors supporting the use of the drug; the left-leaning *Washington Post* emphasized that there are warnings from medical experts about "dangerous consequences" of using it to treat COVID-19.

Of course, polarization is hardly a new phenomenon in the United States. Growing polarization over political values has bled into polarized beliefs about matters of fact, from the relative sizes of Trump's and Obama's inauguration crowds to what the U.S. unemployment rate actually is. And issues of both established and ongoing scientific research are not immune: just consider polarization over global climate change, evolutionary theory, and vaccine safety.

With the arrival of COVID-19, new opportunities for polarization have emerged. Recent surveys have found a stark divide, with Democrats consistently expressing greater concern about the seriousness of COVID-19, while Republicans are more likely to think it is exaggerated. More Democrats report taking precautions, such as avoiding crowds and washing their hands. And these differences seem to extend to specific matters of fact, such as the efficacy of hydroxychloroquine.

Yet with all this polarization, there is still something distinctive and puzzling about these disagreements over COVID-19. Most notable cases of polarization over matters of fact have relatively mild day-to-day consequences. Nobody dies from skepticism about evolution. And while skepticism about global climate change or vaccines may ultimately cause significant harms, long time scales in the first case and herd immunity in the second help to protect nonbelievers from immediate consequences. Given that COVID-19 can kill within a matter of weeks, and that bad choices can put a person in immediate danger, one might think there would not be much room for tribalism. After all, we do not expect polarization over whether, say, drinking antifreeze—or injecting disinfectants, for that matter—is a good idea.

Why are we seeing the polarization over hydroxycholorquine, then, in spite of the serious consequences? The explanation may lie in the kind of information available to the public about COVID-19, which differs importantly from what we see in other cases of polarization about science. When it comes to the health effects of injecting disinfectants, there is no uncertainty about the massive risks. And for that reason, we don't expect polarization to emerge, even if Trump suggests trying it. But even the best information about COVID-19 is in a state of constant flux. Scientists are publishing new articles every day, while old articles and claims are retracted or refuted. Norms of scientific publication, which usually dictate longer time frames and more thorough peer review, have been relaxed by scientific communities desperately seeking solutions. And with readers clamoring for the latest virus news, journalists are on the hunt for new articles they can report on, sometimes pushing claims into prime time before they've been properly vetted.

All this means that there is a huge amount of information circulating that has some scientific legitimacy but that may be dramatically underdeveloped and more likely than normal scientific findings to be overturned. Claims about hydroxychloroquine fall into this category. Despite widely reported but hardly definitive recent studies, which Trump's media critics have latched onto as evidence that hydroxychloroquine does not improve outcomes, the scientific jury is still out. We do not yet know whether hydroxychloroquine, remdesivir, or other possible treatments are effective for COVID-19.

This legitimate uncertainty means that pundits and journalists who treat claims supporting hydroxychloroquine as akin to typical misinformation (or radical conspiracy theories) are misdiagnosing the situation. Trumpeting hydroxychloroquine is undoubtedly risky, both because current evidence is too mixed to support that claim and because it can lead to problems like drug hoarding. But sharing anecdotal accounts of the success of hydroxychloroquine in various clinical settings is not necessarily misinformation—and neither is sharing information about failed clinical trials or shortages for patients who need the drug for other purposes. These are all pieces of evidence that should inform any reasonable person's beliefs about hydroxychloroquine and COVID-19.

THIS IS NOT TO SAY that nothing has gone badly wrong with the public discourse about the drug. Amidst a sea of uncertainty, people are deciding which way to swim by attending to social factors, rather than scientific ones.

Part of the reason this happens is that facts can mislead when they are shared with incomplete context or without other relevant facts. Telling one *isolated* truth, rather than the *whole* truth, can be just as bad as telling a falsehood. This is especially true for issues related to human health, where data is often messy. Some COVID-19 patients who take hydroxychloroquine will recover; some will die. What is difficult to determine is how many who recover would have recovered anyway, and how many who die after taking the drug would have died anyway. In the absence of high-quality studies, determining the proper context for any fact is exceptionally difficult, and even experts struggle to do it well.

The upshot is perhaps counterintuitive: people can wind up misinformed even in the absence of misinformation. Or maybe it is best to think of misinformation as a function of the whole ecology of information available—how it is framed, who shares it, where it gets circulated, and so on—not simply a matter of isolated claims being true or false, more justified or less.

In particular, people become misinformed because they tend to trust those they identify with, meaning they are more likely to listen to those who share their social and political identities. When public figures such as Trump and Rush Limbaugh make claims about hydroxychloroquine, Republicans are more likely to be swayed, while Democrats are not. The two groups then start sharing different sorts of information about hydroxychloroquine, and stop trusting what they see from the other side.

People also like to conform with those in their social networks. It is often psychologically uncomfortable to disagree with our closest friends and family members. But different clusters or cliques can end up conforming to different claims. Some people fit in by rolling their eyes about hydroxychloroquine, while others fit in by praising Trump for supporting it.

These social factors can lead to belief factions: groups of people who share a number of polarized beliefs. As philosophers of science, we have used models to argue that when these factions form, there need not be any underlying logic to the beliefs that get lumped together. Beliefs about the safety of gun ownership, for example, can start to correlate with beliefs about whether there were weapons of mass destruction in Iraq. When this happens, beliefs can become signals of group membership—even for something as dangerous as an emerging pandemic. One person might show which tribe they belong to by sewing their own face mask. Another by throwing a barbeque, despite stay-at-home orders.

And yet another might signal group membership by posting a screed about hydroxychloroquine. There is nothing about hydroxy-chloroquine in particular that makes it a natural talking point for Republicans. It could just as easily have been remdesivir, or one of a half dozen other potential miracle drugs, that was picked up by Fox News, and then by Trump. The process by which Trump settled on hydroxychloroquine was essentially random—and yet, once he began touting it, it became associated with political identity in just the way we have described. (That is not to say that Trump and his media defenders were not on the lookout for an easy out from a growing crisis. Political leaders around the world would love to see this all disappear, irrespective of ideology.)

Sharing encouraging news about possible treatments for a devastating disease is an appropriate thing for political leaders or public health officials to do under many circumstances. But it must be done with utmost care, not only because the informa-tion politicians share may directly influence others' behaviors in dangerous ways, but also because the very fact that a politician or government expert is perceived as representing a particular political tribe can mean their information becomes attached to their positions in preexisting disagreements. The result is that some substantial portion of the population—and in the case of hydroxychloroquine, we still do not know whether it will be Republicans or Democrats—ends up inappropriately skeptical about an important matter of fact.

This tribalism about COVID-19 may be exacerbated by media practices. There is tremendous interest in the disease, and thus tremendous opportunity for journalists to capture readership. Readers are drawn to claims that are surprising and novel, including those that emphasize extreme events. For instance, we see many articles about the most overwhelmed hospitals in the world and the worst-case scenario predictions for COVID-19 deaths, even when many other hospitals in the same regions are not overwhelmed and well-informed predictions of total fatalities vary widely. By contrast, evidence that fits neatly into our current, best theories of COVID-19 is relatively underreported in the mainstream news.

This bias toward extremes means that once opposing camps have formed, there is a lot of fodder for each side to appeal to as evidence of bias. Furthermore, with COVID-19, it is often the case that the different groups only trust one of the extremes. Extremity bias can thus amplify polarization, especially in an already factionalized environment.

The end result is that even without misinformation, or with relatively little of it, we can end up misinformed. And misinformed decision-makers—from patients, to physicians, to public health experts and politicians—will not be able to act judiciously. In the present crisis, this is a matter of life and death.

There are no easy solutions to polarization, writ large. Telling journalists not to report on extreme events is hopeless, though we might do well to call for more nuanced and contextualized reporting —telling the whole truth, rather than some isolated part of it. Politicians, for their part, have plenty of incentives for playing up polarization. But individuals—including physicians and others whose expertise we rely on—can resist, by attempting to recognize the ways that their own belief factions may be distorting the evidence they see and trust. Perhaps more importantly, we must recognize that not everything shared or believed by those with whom we disagree is misinformation, even if it later turns out to have been false.

WILL EVIDENCE-BASED MEDICINE SURVIVE COVID-19?
Trisha Greenhalgh

MAY 29, 2020

COVID-19'S IMPACT has been swift, widespread, and devastating. Never have so many clinicians devoted themselves so resolutely, at significant personal risk, to care for people with a single disease that is not yet in the textbooks. Never have so many scientists worked so fast to generate and summarize research findings in real time. Never have policymakers struggled so hard to apply a complex and contested evidence base to avert an escalating crisis.

And yet, as I write from Oxford, the United Kingdom's daily death toll remains in the hundreds despite weeks of lockdown. In this country at least, we are failing. One of the many issues thrown up by the current confusion is the relationship between research and policy. A leitmotif in the UK government's announcements, in particular, is the claim that they are "following the science." One policy delay after another—testing at ports and airports, quarantining of arrivals from known hotspots, closing schools, banning large gatherings, social distancing, lockdown, controlling outbreaks in care homes, widespread testing, face coverings for the lay public—has been endorsed by the government and its formal advisory bodies only on the grounds that "the evidence base is weak" or even that "the evidence isn't there." The implication is that good policy must wait for good evidence, and in the absence of the latter, inaction is best.

In all of these examples, some evidence in support of active intervention existed at the time the government made the decision not to act. In relation to face coverings, for example, there was basic scientific evidence on how the virus behaves. There were service-level data from hospital and general practitioner records. There were detailed comparative data on the health system and policy responses of different countries. There were computer modeling studies. There was a wealth of anecdotal evidence (for example, one general practitioner reported deaths of 125 patients across a handful of residential care homes). But for the UK government's Scientific Advisory Group for Emergencies (SAGE), whose raison d'être is "ensuring that timely and coordinated scientific advice is made available to decision makers," this evidence carried little weight against the absence of a particular *kind* of evidence—from randomized controlled trials and other so-called "robust" designs.

We could be waiting a very long time and paying a very high human price for the UK government's ultra-cautious approach to "evidence-based" policy. Indeed, I hypothesize that evidence-based medicine—or at least, its exalted position in the scientific pecking order—will turn out to be one of the more unlikely casualties of the COVID-19 pandemic.

THE TERM "EVIDENCE-BASED MEDICINE" was introduced in 1992; it refers to the use of empirical research findings, especially but not exclusively from randomized controlled trials, to inform individual treatment decisions. As a school of medical thinking, it is underpinned by a set of philosophical and methodological assumptions. It embraces an intellectual and social movement with which many are proud to identify. Indeed, I've identified with it myself. I have been involved with the movement from the early 1990s; my book *How to Read a Paper: The Basics of Evidence-Based Medicine and Healthcare* has sold over 100,000 copies and is now in its sixth edition. In my day job at the University of Oxford, I help run the Oxford COVID-19 Evidence Service, producing rapid systematic reviews to assist the global pandemic response, though I've also led some strong critiques of the movement.

Through its highly systematic approach to the production of systematic reviews and the development and dissemination of clinical practice guidelines, evidence-based medicine has saved many lives, including my own. Five years ago I was diagnosed with an aggressive form of breast cancer. I was given three treatments, all of which had been rigorously tested in randomized controlled trials and were included in a national clinical practice guideline: surgery to remove the tumor; a course of chemotherapy; and a drug called Herceptin (a monoclonal antibody against a surface protein being displayed by my cancer cells).

As cancer physician Siddhartha Mukherjee describes in his book *The Emperor of All Maladies* (2010), before randomized controlled trials showed us what worked in different kinds of breast cancer, women were routinely subjected to mutilating operations and dangerous drugs by well-meaning doctors who assumed that "heroic" surgery would help save their lives but which actually contributed to their deaths. With a relatively gentle evidence-based care package, I made a full recovery and have been free of cancer for the past four years. (Incidentally, while going through treatment, I discovered that women who die from breast cancer have often been following quack cures and refusing conventional treatment, so I wrote a book with breast surgeon and fellow breast cancer survivor Liz O'Riordan on how evidence-based medicine saved our lives.)

But as its critical friends have pointed out, evidence-based medicine's assumptions do not always hold. Treatment recommendations based on population averages derived from randomized trials do not suit every patient: individual characteristics must be taken into account. While proponents of evidence-based medicine acknowledged early that explanations from the basic sciences should precede and support empirical trials rather than be replaced by them, the injunction tends to be honored more in the breach than the observance. And as several observers have noted, "preferred" study designs (randomized trials, systematic reviews, and meta-analyses), methodological checklists, and risk-of-bias tools can be manipulated by vested interests, allowing them to brand questionable products and policies as "evidence-based."

In practice, the neat simplicity of an intervention-on versus intervention-off experiment designed to produce a definitive—that is, statistically significant and widely generalizable—answer to a focused question is sometimes impossible. Examples that rarely lend themselves to such a design include upstream preventive public health interventions aimed at supporting widespread and sustained behavior change across an entire population (as opposed to testing the impact of a short-term behavior change in a select sample). In population-wide public health interventions such as diet, alcohol consumption, exercise, recreational drug use, or early-years development, we must not only persuade individuals to change their behavior but also change the environment to make such changes easier to make and sustain.

These system-level efforts are typically iterative, locally grown, and path-dependent, and they have an established methodology for rapid evaluation and adaptation. But because of the longstanding dominance of the evidence-based medicine paradigm, such designs have tended to be classified as a scientific compromise of inherently low methodological quality. While this has been recognized as a problem in public health practice for some time, the inadequacy of the prevailing paradigm has suddenly become mission-critical.

Notwithstanding the oft-repeated cliché that the choice of study design must reflect the type of question (randomized trials, for example, are the preferred design only for therapy questions), many senior scientists interpret evidence-based medicine's hierarchy of evidence narrowly and uncompromisingly. A group convened by the Royal Society recently produced a narrative review on the use of face masks by the general public which incorporated a wide range of evidence from basic science, mathematical modeling, and policy studies. In response, one professor of epidemiology publicly announced:

That is not a piece of research. That is a non-systematic review of anecdotal and non-clinical studies. The evidence we need before we implement public interventions involving billions of people, must come ideally from randomised controlled trials at population level or at least from observational follow-up studies with comparison groups. This will allow us to quantify the positive and negative effects of wearing masks.

This comment, which assigns evidence from experimental trials a more exalted role in policy than the Nobel Prize–winning president of the Royal Society, reveals two unexamined assumptions. First, that the precise quantification of impact from every intervention is both desirable and possible. Second, that the best course of action—both scientifically and morally—is to do nothing until we have definitive findings from a large, comparative study that is unlikely ever to be done. On the contrary, medicine often can and does act more promptly when the need arises.

The principle of acting on partial or indirect evidence, for example, underpins the off-label use of potentially lifesaving medication for new diseases. This happened recently when the U.S. Food and Drug Administration (FDA) issued an emergency use authorization for hydroxychloroquine in patients with severe COVID-19 in certain limited circumstances. Notwithstanding the FDA's own description of the evidence base for this indication as "anecdotal," and reports of harm as well as possible benefit, strong arguments have been made for the cautious prescription of this drug for selected patients with careful monitoring until the results of ongoing trials are available. Nevertheless, criticisms that the FDA's approach was not evidence-based were quick to appear.

IF EVIDENCE-BASED MEDICINE is not the right scientific paradigm for this moment, what is? The framework of complex adaptive systems may be better suited to the analysis of fast-moving infectious diseases.

This paradigm proposes that precise quantification of particular cause-effect relationships in the real world is both impossible (because such relationships are not constant and cannot be meaningfully isolated) and unnecessary (because what matters is what emerges in a particular unique situation). In settings where multiple factors are interacting in dynamic and unpredictable ways, a complex systems approach emphasizes the value of naturalistic methods (where scientists observe and even participate in real-world phenomena, as in anthropological fieldwork) and rapid-cycle evaluation (that is, collecting data in a systematic but pragmatic way and feeding it back in a timely way to inform ongoing improvement). The logic of evidence-based medicine, in which scientists pursued the goals of certainty, predictability, and linear causality, remains useful in some circumstances—for example, the ongoing randomized controlled trials of treatments for COVID-19. But at a public health rather than individual patient level, we need to embrace other epistemic frameworks and use methods to study how best to cope with uncertainty, unpredictability, and nonlinear causality.

The key scientific question about an intervention in a complex system is not "What is the effect size?" or "Is the effect statistically significant, controlling for all other variables?" but "Does this intervention contribute, along with numerous other factors, to a desired outcome in this case?" It is entirely plausible that, as with raising a child, multiple interventions might each contribute to an overall beneficial effect through heterogeneous effects on disparate causal pathways, even though none of these interventions individually would have a statistically significant impact on any predefined variable.

One everyday example of the use of complex causality thinking is the approach used by Dave Brailsford, who was appointed performance director of the British cycling team in the mid 2000s. In a few short years, through changes in everything from the pitch of the saddles to the number of recovery minutes between training intervals, he brought the team from halfway down the world league table to the very top, winning eight of the fourteen gold medals in track and road cycling in the 2008 Beijing Olympics and setting nine Olympic records in London 2012. In Brailsford's words, "The whole principle came from the idea that if you broke down everything you could think of that goes into riding a bike, and then improved it by 1 percent, you will get a significant increase when you put them all together."

There is something to the idea. Marginal gains in a complex system come not just from linear improvements in individual factors but also from synergistic interaction between them. A tiny improvement in an athlete's quality of sleep, say, produces a larger improvement in her ability to sustain an endurance session and even larger improvements in her confidence and speed on the ground.

As Harry Rutter and colleagues explain in a recent article in the *Lancet*, "The Need for a Complex Systems Model of Evidence for Public Health," a similar principle can be applied to public health interventions. Take, for example, the "walking school bus" in which children are escorted to school in a long line, starting at the house of the farthest away and picking up the others on the way. Randomized controlled trials of such schemes have rarely demonstrated statistically significant impacts on predefined health-related outcomes. But a more holistic evaluation demonstrates benefits in all kinds of areas: small improvements in body mass index and fitness, but also extended geographies (the children get to know their own neighborhood better), more positive attitudes toward exercise from parents, parents commenting that children were less tired when they walked to and from school, and children reporting more enjoyment of exercise. Taken together, these marginal gains make the walking school bus an idea worth backing.

To elucidate such complex influences, we need research designs and methods that foreground dynamic interactions and emergence—most notably, in-depth, mixed-method case studies (primary research) and narrative reviews (secondary research) that tease out interconnections and incorporate an understanding of generative causality within the system as a whole.

In a recent paper, David Ogilvie and colleagues argue that rather than considering these two contrasting paradigms as competing and mutually exclusive, they should be brought together. The authors depict randomized trials (what they call the "evidence-based practice pathway") and natural experiments (the "practice-based evidence pathway") not in a hierarchical relationship but in a complementary and recursive one. And they propose that "intervention studies should focus on reducing critical uncertainties, that non-randomized study designs should be embraced rather than tolerated and that a more nuanced approach to appraising the utility of diverse types of evidence is required."

Under a practice-based evidence approach, implementing new policy interventions in the absence of randomized trial evidence is neither back-to-front nor unrigorous. In a fast-moving pandemic, the cost of *inaction* is counted in the grim mortality figures announced daily, but the costs and benefits—both financial and human—of different public health *actions* (lockdown, quarantining arrivals, digital contact tracing) are extremely hard to predict because of interdependencies and unintended consequences. In this context, many scientists, as well as the press and the public, are beginning to question whether evidence-based medicine's linear, cause-and-effect reasoning and uncompromising hierarchy of evidence deserve to remain on the pedestal they have enjoyed for the past twenty-five years.

COVID-19 IS THE BIGGEST COMPARATIVE CASE STUDY of "evidence-based" policymaking the world has ever known. National leaders everywhere face the same threat; their citizens will judge them on how quickly and effectively they contain it. Politicians have listened to different scientists telling different kinds of stories and making different kinds of assumptions. History will soon tell us whether evidence-based medicine's tablets of stone have helped or hindered the public health response to COVID-19.

To reiterate the point I made earlier, there is no doubt that evidence-based medicine has offered and continues to offer powerful insights and still has an important place in the evaluation of therapies. But its principles have arguably been naïvely and indiscriminately overapplied in the current pandemic. The maxim of *primum non nocere*—first, do no harm—may entail that in ordinary medical practice, we should not prescribe therapies until they are justified through a definitive experimental trial. But that narrow interpretation of the Hippocratic principle does not necessarily apply in all contexts, especially when hundreds are dying daily from a disease with no known treatment. On the contrary, it is imperative to try out, with rapid, pragmatic evaluation and iterative improvement cycles, policies that have a plausible chance of working. The definition of good medical and public health practice must be urgently updated.

Greenhalgh

STEPS TO A BETTER COVID-19 RESPONSE
Natalie E. Dean

JULY 30, 2020

HALF A YEAR into the COVID-19 pandemic, more than 150,000 Americans have died from the disease. Over 1 percent of the population has had a confirmed infection, with roughly 90 percent of infections missed. Several other nations have brought transmission under control, but the United States is facing a rapid uptick in the number of new cases. Despite our desperation for life to go back to normal, the end is not yet in sight. How should we think about the ongoing challenge we face?

At this point, we know the problems. The novel coronavirus, SARS-CoV-2, can spread before infected people develop symptoms—between 4 and 41 percent of people never develop symptoms, in fact—yet we are nowhere near herd immunity. At the same time, the United States continues to lack sufficient capacity for testing and contact tracing. Countries such as Germany, Greece, Italy, and Australia conduct, on average, two hundred tests to find a single confirmed case; in the United States, every twelve tests uncover a new infection. Widespread lockdowns imposed in March and April dramatically slowed epidemic growth, but they came with enormous costs, not only economic—leaving tens of millions unemployed—but also social and medical. Vital medical services have been disrupted, including infant vaccination, cancer screening, and HIV treatment programs. The impacts are far-reaching and severe. On the other hand, where lockdowns have been lifted too quickly, transmission has resurged, leading some states to reclose businesses.

It is natural to react to seemingly impossible situations by focusing on the problems. Why is this happening? Why were we so unprepared? Who is to blame? Our collective experience during the pandemic has been likened to the stages of grief; hundreds of millions of people have collectively experienced denial, anger, bargaining, and depression. The last, critical stage is acceptance. Given that the virus is here to stay, how do we learn to live with it safely? This shift in framing may seem simple, but it is important. Energy focused on arguing about problems is energy not spent on developing and implementing solutions.

Of course, characterizing problems can be an important first step in finding answers. Recognizing the role of severe clotting in COVID-19 cases, for example, has helped clinicians to explore antithrombotic treatments. But when it comes to discussion of broader policies, we must be careful not to get stuck at the problem-finding phase. There is clear evidence that the pandemic is disproportionately harming Black, Latinx, and Indigenous communities in the United States. Now that we have identified that problem, what are we doing to fix it? As we continue the work of implementing sorely needed solutions, there are four principles we can use to guide our action.

Be Specific

WE MUST CONSTANTLY WORK to shift the public discussion from the general to the specific, forcing ourselves into the proverbial weeds. Much of the national conversation surrounding lockdowns, for example, has operated at an unhelpful level of generality. Policies of this magnitude have large and broad-reaching impacts—medical and economic, of course, but also legal and social. They are not implemented uniformly, either: they impact different geographic regions and different employment sectors in different ways. The reality is far more complex than a simple dualism: "lockdown good!" or "lockdown bad!"

Moreover, we cannot evaluate the appropriateness of a policy in isolation without a clearly defined alternative. The value of many "exit plans" that have been reported on is their specificity and detail—the pains they take to indicate fine points and to search for proactive strategies that can replace harsher restrictions without putting populations at an unacceptable level of risk. A similar framing for our discussions around school reopening is useful. The options we have do not fall neatly into two poles, distance learning versus a pre-pandemic return to schools. What does social distancing for elementary school students look like? Can some instruction be moved outside? How can indoor activities be conducted more safely? The act of laying out alternatives is instructive, as it gives us something concrete to debate.

In examining specifics, our strategies need not only be about reducing COVID-19 infections and deaths. They can also be about minimizing the broader impacts of the pandemic. Schools provide many critical services to our communities, for example—not just education, of course, but also meal programs. Where schools have closed, some areas have continued to make regular meals available for pick up, thus mitigating one of the consequences of this particular policy. Another example is the interruption of routine medical care like cancer screening and infant vaccination. As some patients are reluctant to visit hospitals for fear of infection, patients may prefer decentralized care at remote offices, or even home-based care. By breaking diffuse larger problems into specific smaller problems, a seemingly intractable problem becomes more manageable.

Compare Globally

AS WE CONTINUE to search for solutions, we would be wise to look globally. Each country, with its own unique circumstances, is tackling the same basic set of challenges. This generates a wealth of data points for us to study and lessons we can learn from alternative approaches. A shift from hospital-based to home-based care was an early lesson from northern Italy's outbreak, for example, as described in a case study comparing hard-hit Lombardy with neighboring Veneto.

One element of this is considering the areas that are having the greatest success and trying to learn from them. Even if New Zealand has the epidemiological advantage of geographic isolation, what can we learn from the clear crisis communications employed by Prime Minister Jacinda Ardern? Likewise, what can we take away from the massive testing campaigns conducted in China? Following its

2015 Middle East Respiratory Syndrome (MERS) outbreak, South Korea dramatically improved its early detection surveillance systems and infection prevention protocols. In Japan emphasis has been on reducing close-range conversations in crowded places (3Cs) and focused detection of large transmission clusters using teams of public health nurses. In South Africa community health care workers have gone door-to-door to ask about symptoms and raise awareness. In Kerala, India, housing and meals have been provided to stranded migrant workers. Dedicated hotlines and apps in Vietnam have kept the public up to date on the latest information. The Democratic Republic of the Congo has repurposed contact tracing protocols originally developed for Ebola.

Some have sensibly taken a systematic approach to learning from other countries. On the website Our World in Data, readers can study Exemplars in Global Health to learn from South Korea, Vietnam, and Germany about their successful COVID-19 responses. In April the UK's Royal Society of scientists launched the DELVE (Data Evaluation and Learning for Viral Epidemics) initiative, whereby multidisciplinary teams gather evidence from other countries and synthesize these into detailed reports and policy recommendations. Its May report on test, trace, isolate compared policies across successful countries to identify commonalities. It highlighted the short turnaround times of testing results and the use of apps to supplement manual tracing by performing automated follow-up symptom checks. Importantly, for test, trace, isolate, and for other policies, not all countries have pursued the same approach. This diversity of response demonstrates that the same playbook is not needed everywhere.

Think Local

ONCE WE HAVE IDENTIFIED strategies to pursue, we must think carefully about how to make them work in local conditions. Adaptation is critical; not all solutions will work equally well everywhere. Drive-through testing sites may work well in Ohio, for example, but not in New York City. In neighborhoods with many undocumented immigrants, traced contacts may not want to share personal information. One-size-fits-all solutions do not exist, and top-down approaches can falter when unexpected problems arise in implementation. Mathematical models can help us anticipate how quickly labs need to turn around test results, how many contacts need to be traced, and how many need to adhere to quarantine, but they do not tell us how to reach this level of success.

To tailor strategies to the local context, we must look for solutions from within—that is, from those doing the most successful work in the field: the contact tracers no one hangs up on, the nursing homes with no outbreaks. To figure out how these outliers have succeeded, the best approach is to engage those on the front lines. Incorporating team members at all levels in the solution can yield the most creative ideas, and it also helps to ensure the whole team is invested in carrying these ideas forward. This approach can yield generalizable lessons, such as improving caller ID so that more people answer calls from contact tracers, but for many other problems there will be no quick fixes.

Contact tracing, in particular, relies heavily on the skills of interviewers to earn trust of patients so that they feel comfortable sharing important but sensitive information. A successful tracer may have a particular way of structuring the interview, or even use a particular tone of voice. Outside consultants can facilitate but not replace the learning process. Rather than being told what works, participants benefit from the discovery process itself—measuring performance, finding the outliers, and seeing firsthand what makes them more effective. This is what can inspire lasting change.

Build to Learn

FINALLY, we need to create an architecture for learning—a plan for gathering insights to inform our evidence-based decisions. Over the last several months, many online tools have sprung up to help us monitor the data, including the COVID Tracking Project, COVID Act Now, COVID Exit Strategy, and Johns Hopkins Testing Insights Initiative, to name only a few. These reporting dashboards give us a way to assess at a glance what is going on across the country, but can be undermined by missing data across the reported metrics. Statistics are generally provided at the state level rather than the preferred county or zip code level. Furthermore, they are rarely broken out by age and race or ethnicity, primarily because states have not adopted a standardized format for reporting. A simple example is how data are broken out into age categories. Where age ranges are defined differently—where one state lumps people in the 18–34 age bucket but another uses the range 18–49, say—they cannot be compared in a meaningful way. Without standardization that enables data to be combined, we are not getting full use of the data that our clinical and public health teams work hard to collect.

Contact tracing is another extraordinarily valuable learning tool. By identifying the likely source of infections, we have a data-driven way to evaluate the riskiness of different activities. For example, though we have evidence that transmission clusters are linked to nightclubs, churches, and Zumba classes, there remains uncertainty about movie theaters, subways, and airplanes. Finding a safe path forward involves identifying low-risk venues as much as about identifying high-risk venues. With businesses reopening or implementing new mitigation measures, the landscape of settings we need to examine is constantly changing. We need greater investment in time and resources to collect and study complex tracing data to generate new and actionable insights, so that we can continue to learn as our lifestyles evolve.

Prospective cohort studies, where populations are carefully studied over time, can generate very high-quality evidence. As these studies take time to set up, we need to start planning now for the information we want to have in the future. This effort can pay dividends, though, in that the results are more likely to be definitive. At the start of the pandemic, some complained that randomized clinical trials of different COVID-19 treatments were too slow and that therapies should be approved on limited evidence. Still, those who forged ahead with randomized trials produced high-quality data that produced both wins (the steroid dexamethasone) and losses (the antimalarial hydroxychloroquine).

Not all policy questions can be addressed in a randomized trial, of course. While Norwegian researchers proposed a randomized study of school reopening, it was not approved by the government. But the act of describing what such a trial would look like—the alternatives being compared, the key outcomes to measure—moves the conversation forward. And where randomized studies may not be feasible, we must pursue a range of well-designed observational cohort studies as the next best option.

UNLIKE PROBLEM-BASED THINKING, which looks back on—and often gets stuck in—the past, solution-based thinking looks forward to a safer and healthier future for all. It welcomes even incremental improvements as moving us closer to this goal. And it rejects the wishful thinking that holds out for a simple fix, such as a vaccine. Scientists are working tirelessly to develop, test, and manufacture a safe form of immunization, but meanwhile there is so much more we can and must do to protect our communities. Increase testing capacity, eliminate bottlenecks, scale up contact tracing, increase mask wearing, improve public health messaging, and carefully study the data to inform targeted policies—all these have an essential and urgent role to play, even after months of lost opportunities. We must not give in to the pressure to oversimplify the conversation or rest content with false dichotomies.

In the end, we need more emphasis on what Devi Sridhar, chair of global public health at the University of Edinburgh, has called the "hard slog of public health" and less on silver bullets, in part because waiting for some future panacea may deter us from learning how to do things better now. It is thanks to the public health slog, for example, that millions in Africa are now receiving lifesaving antiretroviral therapy at thousands of community care sites in the aftermath of the explosive HIV epidemic in the early 2000s. As a result, for so many HIV is a chronic illness rather than a death sentence. For COVID-19, the countries that are doing the best right now worked hard to achieve their results, and it is because their communities feel safe that they are closest to the "normal" we desire. Solution-based thinking involves rolling up our sleeves to put in the hard work needed to get us there—and appreciating why this hard work on the small details is worthwhile.

Dean

HOW A POPULAR MEDICAL DEVICE ENCODES RACIAL BIAS

Amy Moran-Thomas

AUGUST 5, 2020

COVID-19 CARE has brought the pulse oximeter into many U.S. homes. This compact medical device, costing as little as $20, clips onto a fingertip and helps gauge how much oxygen is making it to the blood. When COVID-19 fevers moved through my household earlier this year, everything suddenly revolved around the number on its tiny screen, which reports oxygen saturation as a percentage. Normal readings are in the range of 95 to 100 percent; my husband could only sleep if I stayed up to make sure his readings didn't plummet into the 70s again. Our doctor said to go back to the hospital if the device's reading dropped to 92 and stayed there, but most nights it hovered along that edge. I began to wonder exactly what this object was telling us.

To picture what's happening inside a pulse ox—as health care providers call it—start by thinking about what's happening inside your body. Blood saturated with oxygen is bright crimson thanks to iron-containing hemoglobin, which picks up the gas molecules from your lungs to deliver them to your organs. In the absence of oxygen, the same hemoglobin dims to a cold purple-red. The oximeter detects this chromatic chemistry by shining two lights through your finger—one infrared, one red—and sensing how much comes through on the other side. Oxygen-saturated hemoglobin absorbs more infrared light and also allows more red light to pass through than its deoxygenated counterpart. Adjusting for certain technicalities using your pulse, the device reads out the color of your blood several times a second.

To "see" your blood, though, the light must pass through your skin. This should give us pause, since a range of technologies based on color-sensing are known to reproduce racial bias. Photographic film calibrated for white skin, for example, often created distorted images of nonwhite people until its built-in assumptions started to be acknowledged and reworked in the 1970s; traces of racial biases remain in photography still today. Similar disparities have surfaced around several health devices, including Fitbits. How had designers managed to avoid such problems in the case of the oximeter, I wondered? As I dug deeper, I couldn't find any record that the problem ever was fully fixed. Most oximeters on the market today were initially calibrated primarily for light skin, and they still often reproduce subtle errors for nonwhite people.

In medical and technology communities, there is a perception that this bias isn't a big deal. To understand why, I reached out to manufacturers, doctors, researchers, and government regulators to ask for any updates to these previously documented issues. Many responded along these lines: "The errors haven't really been dealt with, but here's why it doesn't matter." Others thought the stories that get told about the harmlessness of racial disparities reveal the very opposite: unequal standards that have become normalized. It all matters—the errors, the history that produced them, the future they're being built into, and the justifications about racism they reveal in U.S. science and medicine.

IN 2005 A TEAM OF PHYSICIANS studied oximetry's racial bias in critical detail. The group often works at the famous mountaintop Hypoxia Lab, founded at the University of California, San Francisco (UCSF) by John Severinghaus, inventor of blood gas analysis, who did foundational work in medical devices for anesthesiology. "In our eighteen years of testing pulse oximeter accuracy," the team noted in its article, "the majority of subjects have been light skinned. . . . Most pulse oximeters have probably been calibrated using light-skinned individuals, with the assumption that skin pigment does not matter."

But after hearing about a range of "unacceptable errors in pulse oximetry" among Black wearers, the UCSF study was "specifically designed to determine whether errors at low [arterial oxygen saturation] correlate with skin color." Since errors don't tend to show up at healthy oxygen levels, a special protocol is necessary to check accuracy at lower oxygen, which better simulates an actual health crisis. The doctors collected readings with a range of people using several pulse ox models, then checked their readings against a different kind of test based on arterial blood gas, the "gold standard" test for oxygen levels. (The latter measure is more invasive, requiring blood from an artery, which is why the pulse ox is often used as a proxy in hospitals.)

Crosschecking these two measures over 1,067 data points, the team found a clear pattern of errors. For nonwhite people, the machines mostly tended to overestimate saturation levels by several points. The study only included participants who identified as Black or white, but the authors noted that degrees of errors have also been observed among Latinx, Indigenous, and many other nonwhite people. The team's follow-up study, published in 2007, focused on safety errors for people with "intermediate" skin tones and included a larger group of women. This more detailed data again found a clear pattern: pulse ox "bias was generally the greatest in dark-skinned subjects, intermediate for intermediate skin tones, and least for lightly pigmented individuals." Racial errors grew significant at lower oxygen levels, starting around 90 and growing widest in the 70s.

In principle, the implications can be troubling. The night we first got a pulse ox, my husband woke up with his oxygen at 77. In their studies of that low saturation range, the UCSF doctors noticed "a bias of up to 8 percent . . . in individuals with darkly pigmented skin," errors that "may be quite significant under some circumstances." Thus, for a nonwhite person, a reading of 77 like my husband's could hide a true saturation as low as 69—even greater immediate danger. But EMTs or intake nurses might not be able to detect those discrepancies during triage. The number appears objective and race-neutral.

Indeed, while the oximeter is a key tool for some patients in deciding when to *go* to the hospital, it's also what they use *at* the hospital. Clinical guidance about giving oxygen tends to be loosely keyed to a certain threshold of oxygen saturation; protocols recommend particular interventions at 88, 90, and 92 percent, for example. Racial errors in these higher saturation ranges tend to be narrower disparities of 1–4 percentage points, but they still can mislead if they go undetected. In particular situations, another study notes, errors of that margin "may severely affect the treatment decisions in borderline cases."

This might seem like a fine point, but medicine is made of fine points that turn into ordinary decisions. The UCSF data shows that three brands of pulse oximeters (Nonin, Nellcor, and Masimo) demonstrate clear variability around one of the most common clinical decision points: a reading of 88 percent. Pulse ox readings can also be affected by conditions such as anemia, jaundice, poor circulation, and nail polish. Physicians in a clinic may not distinguish errors stemming from an underlying condition and those caused by the device's bias on darker skin. The UCSF lab data are revealing on this point. The study participants were "healthy, nonsmoking" Black and white young people in their twenties and thirties, mostly UCSF medical students, none of whom "had lung disease, obesity, or cardiovascular problems." This pool of participants allowed the researchers to isolate skin color calibration errors alone, eliminating misreadings due to underlying comorbidities.

Most hospital protocols now recommend starting oxygen at 90. Below that threshold, damage to vital organs such as the heart, brain, lungs, and kidneys becomes an immediate danger. In a mixed general population, a true blood oxygen saturation of 88 percent would, on average, produce a pulse ox reading of 89 to 90 using the most common meter in hospitals. In that case, guidelines would correctly suggest going on oxygen. But Black patients, equally in crisis at 88, would get an average reading of 91—just above the intervention threshold.

Physicians disagree on the clinical significance of these discrepancies. Do slight racial errors really matter in practice? Like any vital sign, pulse ox readings are one among many factors considered when making a critical care decision. Most caregivers I spoke to noted that a nurse or doctor on careful watch, drawing on a range of other information, would use their training to pick out patterns and place numbers in broader context alongside a patient's perceived sense of distress. One critical care specialist told me she felt that the errors found by the UCSF studies would not change the care that patients with darker skin receive where she worked. I could imagine how that may be true in particular cases such as hers, but no one had collected reassuring evidence about the topic at her hospital—much less nationally or globally—so I found myself staring at the disquieting graphs of the only systematic data available as she told anecdotes about how she would contextualize such readings. I hung up the phone feeling unsettled by her words: there was "usually" no way this could matter, she said. Her insights helped me formulate a more elusive question: What about those moments that fall outside *usually*?

In my own experience this spring, the hospital's pulse ox gave a reading of 91 exactly as I arrived at the ER with trouble breathing. I was told that around 90 might mean I needed oxygen, while 91 meant wait and see. This seemed to be the rule of thumb in use, though it did not appear hard and fast. I did not receive crosschecks such as an arterial blood gas test. Such procedures are much more common in critical care units, but 95 percent of people coping with coronavirus today never end up there. The ER nursing team around me seemed to be looking at the pulse ox numbers very closely. They were wary about the "happy hypoxia" associated with COVID-19. Before long my oxygen came up a few points and I was sent home, still with difficulty breathing, now with instructions to keep isolating and buy a pulse ox. I am white, and these calls worked out. But a Black person with the same pulse ox reading at intake could have been at or below the threshold to get oxygen. How would anyone have known for sure?

These concerns don't end with clinical practice, either. Medicare reimbursement also uses pulse ox measures as key thresholds, with much less nuance than a nurse or doctor. At a reading of 88 or 89, Medicare will reimburse for oxygen at home, but at 90 it won't. In effect, this means people with darker skin may have to be sicker in order to qualify for the same treatment as people with white skin. This could lead to delays in recovery, worse outcomes, and greater likelihoods of future comorbidities as patients wait for the meter to catch up to bodily realities.

SOME CAREGIVERS I SPOKE WITH sounded exhausted to field questions about pulse ox biases. They were beleaguered, no doubt, by a thousand other COVID-19 contingencies and more obvious manifestations of inequities. Even if they had never noticed glitches, it could be painful to wonder. Others I spoke to argued that any racial discrepancies at all were simply unacceptable. When people rely on devices for a snapshot, just as with Kodak film, shouldn't everyone's picture be equally clear? Anything less widens room for mistakes that may amplify existing inequalities. It creates a situation where hospital care teams need to work *around* the subtle racial biases of their tools.

"How is racism operating here?" Physician, epidemiologist, and civil rights activist Camara Phyllis Jones urges health practitioners to ask this question throughout their work. In the case of pulse oximetry, errors of slight degrees mean a lot more than they otherwise might because of the larger patterns of inadvertent racism in hospitals they plug into. Nonwhite patients are already more likely to have identical signs classified as less urgent by physicians, as decades of research documenting unintentional medical racism shows. Measurement errors falsely indicating that hospitalized patients are safer than they are could further contribute to suboptimal care. As caregivers argue, "Any decision making rooted in implicit bias is detrimental" when "an incorrect assumption could literally mean the difference between life and death."

Amid problems with unreliable testing for COVID-19, for example, some patients of color report being dismissed from the ER by doctors attributing their difficulty breathing to anxiety. In fact, in the name of combatting known treatment disparities in ERs, the Association of American Medical Colleges suggests hospitals "remove as much individual discretion as possible," instead seeking "objective measures" to help doctors overcome "implicit biases that providers don't even know they have." In reality, the policy could further amplify the problem in cases where seemingly objective measures themselves display hidden racial bias. What happens when efforts to overcome physician bias rely on devices that are also biased?

On top of this, pulse ox data is a key vital sign being fed into the algorithms that increasingly guide hospital decisions. As reported in *Nature* and *Science*, many algorithms already suggest inadequate care along patterned racial divides: patients of color have to be sicker, on average, in order to receive the same interventions as white patients. They are less likely to be promptly identified for ICU admission, even with otherwise identical profiles. Yet algorithmic tools such as the EPIC "Deterioration Index" can only aspire to be as good as the instruments feeding data into them. With pulse ox disparities, what are machines learning from these distorted inputs? The proprietary EPIC Early Warning equation incorporates the Rothman Index, and half of the eight cut-off numbers for oxygen saturation built into that measure are in the range for racial errors. Like the problems magnified by "the coded gaze" of algorithms elsewhere, even small racial disparities could amplify unequal outputs.

Beyond the pulse ox alone, this also matters for other wearable chromatic devices and the algorithms they feed. Pretending that they are colorblind can further amplify how, as a recent article in *Scientific American* put it, "Racism, Not Genetics, Explains Why Black Americans Are Dying of COVID-19." I called my colleague from MIT's Little Devices Lab, Jose Gomez-Marquez, whose research involves prying open devices to understand their inner workings. He always knows the latest med-tech rumors, and I wanted to ask if there was some inside story about recalibrating oximeters more recently. Had there been some quiet racial justice work that already made corrections for its biased design?

None that he'd heard of, Jose said. Oximeters predated much of the current DIY digital medical technology scene, developed across Europe, North America, and Japan decades ago. Among makers today, the device is often considered simple to the point of being child's play, in comparison to the cutting-edge spaces where most groups compete for prestigious breakthroughs and lucrative markets.

For devices shaped by "discriminatory design," as sociologist of science and technology Ruha Benjamin calls it, inequalities that are not intentional can still produce patterned exclusions and unequal rates of survival. The UCSF doctors who documented these disparities suggested "built-in user-optional adjustments" be designed into future models. But more than a decade later, I couldn't find any examples on the market. The doctors also concluded that, at bare minimum, "warning labels should be provided to users, possibly with suggested correction factors." I checked the box my pulse ox came in, but it only had fine print about inaccuracies linked to dark nail polish.

When I reached out to the team behind those breakthrough UCSF studies fifteen years ago—Philip Bickler and John Feiner—they confirmed that they had not yet seen evidence of the change they hoped for around this issue. Bickler—now chief of neuroanesthesia, UCSF professor, and collaborating director of the Hypoxia Lab—said that as far as he was aware, "Manufacturers, as a group, have not responded at all adequately to this problem." He notes that he views the current state of oximetry as a "great example of a bias in medical technology that disenfranchises a huge percentage of the earth's population," which especially worries him with "COVID-19 disproportionately affecting Black and Latinx populations."

One pulse ox manufacturer, Nonin, sought to address race-based errors in its devices back in the 2000s. A page of its website explains its work so far in comparison to its larger competitors. Several other companies in the original study also replied to my questions, but none provided data showing the problem has been fixed. I combed through published studies they pointed to for context. The most widely quoted was a study from 2017, which several companies presented as a bright spot showing that oximetry readings were not racially biased among thirty-five infants. (Other studies have shown that babies' low melanin production and the much thinner microstructure of newborn skin leave them less susceptible to chromatic measures' racial bias.) This is reassuring news for infant ICUs, but it does not tell us the device errors have been fixed for others: the study itself notes standing disparities for adults.

One of the largest manufacturers said it had reassuring internal data for one specific line of models, but that response left me wondering about the many other models it sells to hospitals today. Companies should create public-facing record and global historical memory of any such corrective work that already happened, behind the scenes of our health systems' privatized patchworks, to let us all know clearly where things stand. After all, these are not new questions: while COVID-19 gives new emphasis to the pulse ox, the device has long been crucial for treating respiratory conditions with their own histories of chronic racial biases in diagnosis and care.

At present, there seems to be little consensus among doctors, too, about what to make of the available studies, including those cited in 2019 textbooks on the need to correct for devices' racial errors. One such study still being reprinted from 1990 recounts data showing the pulse ox target used for white patients on ventilators, 92, often resulted in hypoxia for Black patients; for this patient group, a pulse ox reading of 95 corresponded to an arterial blood gas reading of 92. Yet several doctors I checked with said they never learned this, even back in 1990. Should health care providers be aware of these significant errors, or are textbooks teaching doctors outdated corrections that could also potentially do harm by leading to confusion or wrong adjustments? Companies should be transparent, assessing and clarifying any margins of racial bias on their websites, because getting this wrong in either direction could amplify racial care disparities.

UNTIL THEN, the pulse ox could be read as a case study of systemic racism in miniature—a nexus where, as anthropologists note, black boxes and public secrets often go hand in hand. Since the original UCSF study ended with a call to action, it is disturbing to track its afterlife in the medical literature and within the contours of the present pandemic. Later studies citing the UCSF work often imply the bodies of nonwhite people are to blame for making the device malfunction. Most recently, one 2020 study attributed race-based pulse ox errors to "co-morbidities upon which the device is used." But the participants in that study had no underlying medical conditions; they were healthy young Black people.

In the 1990s, the Food and Drug Administration (FDA) stopped allowing all-white male study samples. But *mostly* white study samples are still the norm; current guidelines suggest including at least two people with "darkly pigmented" skin in a group otherwise 85 percent white. Yet this can still obscure errors due to racial bias, by allowing those few participants' data points to be cast as outer clusters in white-centric safety standards. As Sara Ahmed, a scholar of institutional cultures, explains, this type of structure for "being included" still reproduces and recasts the norms of an unmarked white center, "against which others appear as points of deviation."

One early literature review commenting on pulse ox racial bias, for example, highlighted several studies showing "significantly more signal quality problems" for Black patients. It also covered one study that did not find any bias—but the reviewers noted that the last study only included four Black patients in a group of twenty-one subjects, so "the population size was probably too small to show up minor differences in pulse oximetry performance." That study, critiqued as inconclusive to assess bias because it had under-sampled people of color back in 1991, included the exact ratio of nonwhite participants that the FDA guidelines still recommend including today.

The UCSF studies provided an illuminating alternative model to correct such issues: by collecting data for equal-sized subgroups, they broke the numbers down to check whether it was equally safe for each group. This showed something the FDA study designs had worryingly missed: the most common oximeters in U.S. hospitals at the time did not meet FDA thresholds of safety for people with darker skin. When those data points get blended into mostly white statistics, the data may look fine. In this, the pulse ox is also a microcosm for the problems facing our democracy. *Equal* safety does not mean majority-fits-all.

These devices' subtle inequities are also haunted by much deeper histories of racism in science and medicine. During the time when corporations rose from plantations, machines to measure breathing were designed to quantify—and *justify*—racial hierarchies. These orders were built on the idea that darker skin color itself was a co-morbidity. Medical doctors of the era argued that violent regimes of Black enslavement and Indigenous dispossession were not unjust because they held important health benefits for the supposedly inherently dysfunctional biologies of nonwhite people. Certain devices to measure breathing became part of larger machines to keep people in place, as historian Lundy Braun shows in her work on this medical legacy. This is part of larger patterns that scholars such as Dorothy Roberts and Anne Fausto-Sterling show get continuously encoded into medical school curricula and scientific health research taken to be cutting-edge. Even today, in many clinics, the spirometer often has a "race button" as a legacy of this disturbing history.

Oximeters, by contrast, were first conceived to monitor and protect the breathing capacities of those with privileged mobility. It is no coincidence that novelist Esi Edugyan imagined freedom's trajectory as a hot air balloon ride over a sugar plantation: in fact, the idea for oximetry began at that height. Hot air balloon experiments in the 1800s led to the development of blood oxygen saturation measures after scientist-adventurers became paralyzed while airborne, as made famous across Europe and the Americas by scientist Paul

Bert's studies of the *Zenith* (though the pulse oximeter as known to-day wouldn't be realized until decades later, by Takuo Aoyagi). Now crucial to the practice of anesthesiology, the device was initially most popular among those able to reach high altitude: pilots, astronauts, mountaineers. Oximetry's origins came from the sciences of safety for white flight, and pulse oximeters still protect people unevenly against a virus that causes difficulty breathing, in ways that some experts liken to falling oxygen at high altitude.

There is no reason to build these disparities into the next generation of technologies. Yet that is exactly what will happen if we don't take active steps to remove existing racial biases. The pulse ox's unequal metrics are one among countless converging factors that stack the deck against nonwhite people facing systemic inequities. Yet there will never be one single reset button for history, activists remind us; the hard work ahead is tackling each facet of such inequity as it comes into view. Rather than *normalized* inequalities, the pulse ox could become a case study in everyday repair work, as Toni Morrison calls it—small, material, mundane practices in the direction of justice. In the face of vastly unfinished racial reckoning and historical repair, it matters all the more to do the work of investing in the small chances for concrete action right now in our hands.

Engineers at MIT, for example, say adding adjustable LED lights to pulse oximeters could enable devices to set individualized baselines for each wearer, tailoring accuracy and fostering equitable safety. The technical capacity already exists. Funding from the National Institutes of Health could help fast-track long overdue corrections as part of a broad consortium coming together to fix this problem, to share progress so far and resources moving forward. With COVID-19 death tolls already over 160,000 in the United States alone and rising daily, the pulse ox is a vital tool for survival. It should not work least accurately for those whose health is most in danger.

These patterned errors are disturbingly symbolic traces of whose safety our institutions and technologies were built for, leaving people of color to hope that less than equal will be good enough. Truly rethinking collective safety and justice means teaching the next generation—and trying to learn ourselves—how to build worlds that don't normalize *any* margin of error that would disproportionately obfuscate patients' vital signs based on the color of their skin. Each moment until this work exists, oximeters remain another disturbing materialization of how white supremacy has been built into our systems and infrastructures of perception—even programmed into the very machines we rely on to quantify danger when someone can't breathe.

CONTRIBUTORS

Sarah Burgard is Professor of Sociology and, by courtesy, Epidemiology and Public Policy at the University of Michigan, where she directs the Population Studies Center.

Alex de Waal is Executive Director of the World Peace Foundation at the Fletcher School at Tufts University. His latest book, *New Pandemics, Old Politics: Two Hundred Years of the War on Disease and Its Alternatives*, will be published in spring 2021.

Natalie E. Dean is Assistant Professor of Biostatistics at the University of Florida.

Jonathan Fuller is a medical doctor and Assistant Professor of History and Philosophy of Science at the University of Pittsburgh.

Jeremy A. Greene is William H. Welch Professor of Medicine and the History of Medicine and Director of the Institute of the History of Medicine at Johns Hopkins University. He practices medicine at East Baltimore Medical Center. His most recent book is *Generic: The Unbranding of Modern Medicine.*

Trisha Greenhalgh is a medical doctor and Professor of Primary Care Health Sciences at the University of Oxford, where she codirects the Interdisciplinary Research in Health Sciences Unit.

John P. A. Ioannidis is Professor of Medicine, Epidemiology and Population Health, Biomedical Data Science (by courtesy), and Statistics (by courtesy) at Stanford University. He codirects the Meta-Research Innovation Center at Stanford (METRICS).

Lucie Kalousova is Assistant Professor of Sociology at the University of California, Riverside.

Marc Lipsitch is Professor of Epidemiology at the Harvard T. H. Chan School of Public Health and director of the Center for Communicable Disease Dynamics.

Amy Moran-Thomas is Alfred Henry and Jean Morrison Hayes Career Development Associate Professor of Anthropology at MIT. She is author of *Traveling with Sugar: Chronicles of a Global Epidemic.*

Cailin O'Connor is Associate Professor of Logic and Philosophy of Science at the University of California, Irvine. She is coauthor, with James Owen Weatherall, of *The Misinformation Age: How False Beliefs Spread*.

Dóra Vargha is Senior Lecturer in Medical Humanities at the University of Exeter. She is author of *Polio across the Iron Curtain: Hungary's Cold War with an Epidemic*.

James Owen Weatherall is Professor of Logic and Philosophy of Science at the University of California, Irvine. He is coauthor, with Cailin O'Connor, of *The Misinformation Age: How False Beliefs Spread*.

Jonathan White is Deputy Head of the European Institute and Professor of Politics at the London School of Economics.